New York City

Interactive Travel Guide and Zombie Survival Game
By John Pennington

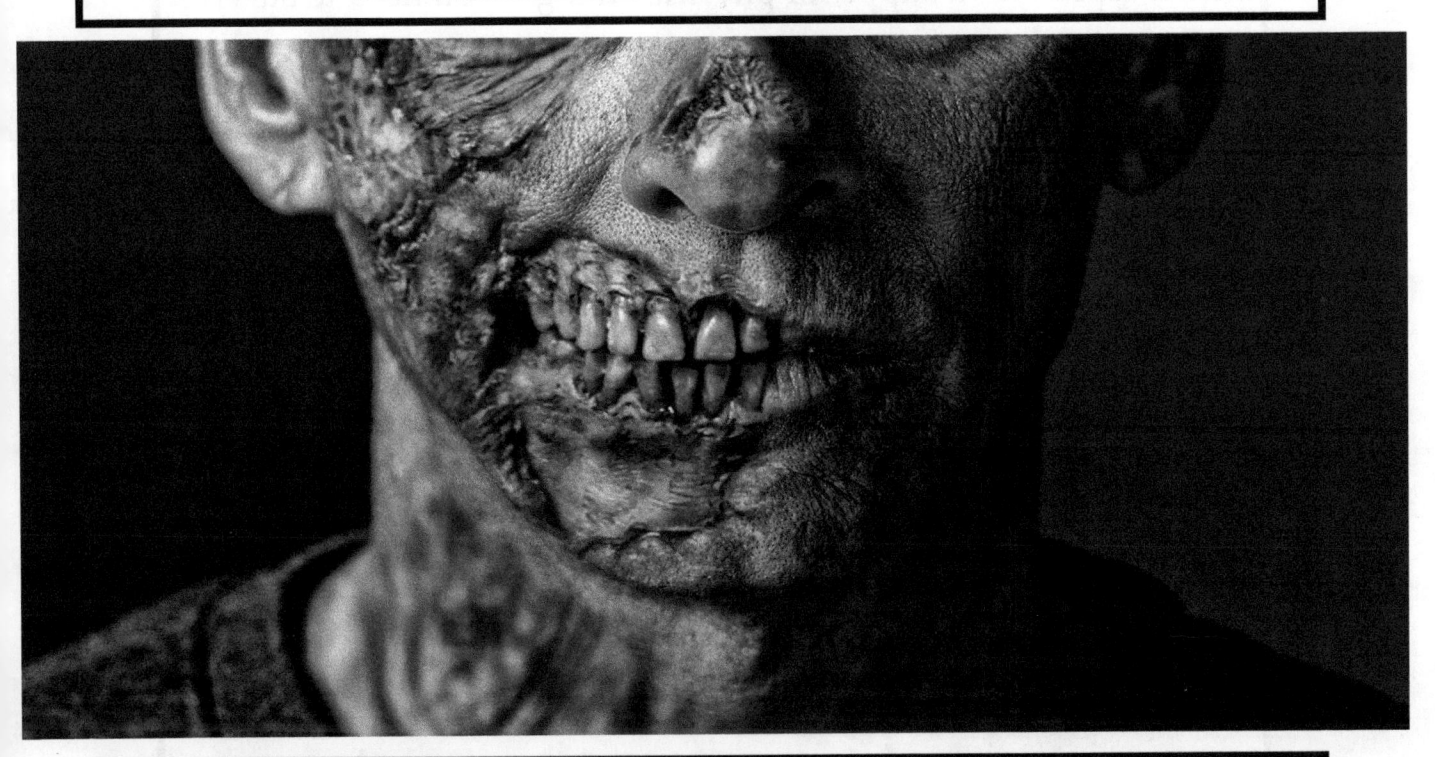

Dates:_____ Humanity Score:_____

This guide provides a fun way to explore a new city and some easy to access information on historic locations, food, entertainment and more.

As you explore the city you can also play the live action zombie survival game included. Collect a score, items and try to survive.

This guide focuses on free and low cost activities over expensive.

Can you survive your trip? Keep those brains protected!

Have fun!

How to use this book:

You will keep track of three categories as you explore. Food, Energy and Humanity.

Food represents a supply of physical strength you need to survive your exploration. You will use one "food" for every location you visit. Obtaining more "food" can be accomplished at every "food" location you visit.

Energy represents a supply of mental strength you need to survive your exploration. You will use one "Energy" for every location you visit. Obtaining more "Energy" can be accomplished at every "Energy" location you visit.

Humanity represents your ability to rescue items that you want to survive the zombie apocalypse. "Humanity" represents your SCORE or the success of your trip. These items can be located at any "Humanity" location you visit.

Examples of Locations:

Food: Restaurant, café, bakery, snack bar, dinner, food truck, vending machine, food court, etc.

Energy: Dance club, toy store, arcade, clothing store, theater, concert hall, park bench, etc.

Humanity: Historic location, book store, museum, comic book convention, etc.

*many locations can serve multiple purposes. In order to take advantage of this fact you must make a listing for all categories you wish to use.

Example: A museum might fit the category for "Humanity" (I will save this historic artifact), "Energy" (this location is fun), and "Food" (this location has a food court.

How to play:

1. Visit a location

2. Determine that locations category (food, energy, humanity)

3. Clear the Zombies! This is accomplished by getting the "Zombies" name (signature, autograph, or print). Consider this a chance to get to know people. If you want you can get some zombie or brain stickers or stamps for them.

4. Collect the reward. Your reward is equal to the number of names recorded. Humanity allows you to take one item for every "Zombie" named. 3 names equal 3 reward items of the location type.

5. When the trip is over you can record your total "humanity" score on the front page.

Record Sheet

Food: (Start with 6)

Energy: (Start with 6)

Humanity Items Sheet (items you saved on your trip)

Location Suggestions (food) (low cost)

Prisillo Italian Panini

Coffee Project New York

Los Tacos

L'industric Pizzeria

Little Collins

Periscope Coffee

Bleecker Street Pizza

Ruffian Wine Bar and Chef's Table

Pizza Suprema

La Contenta

Times Square Diner

Mountain Province

Café Habana

Pita Palace

The Halal Guys

Los Mariscos

Westway Diner

Location Suggestions (Energy/Humanity)

Central Park

Metropolitan Museum of Art

Empire State Building

Statue of Liberty

Grand Central Station

Broadway

Bryant Park

St. Patrick's Cathedral

Staten Island Ferry

Radio City Music Hall

Rockefeller Center

Madison Square Garden

Times Square

Fifth Avenue

Chelsea Market

Ellis Island

Greenwich village

Soho

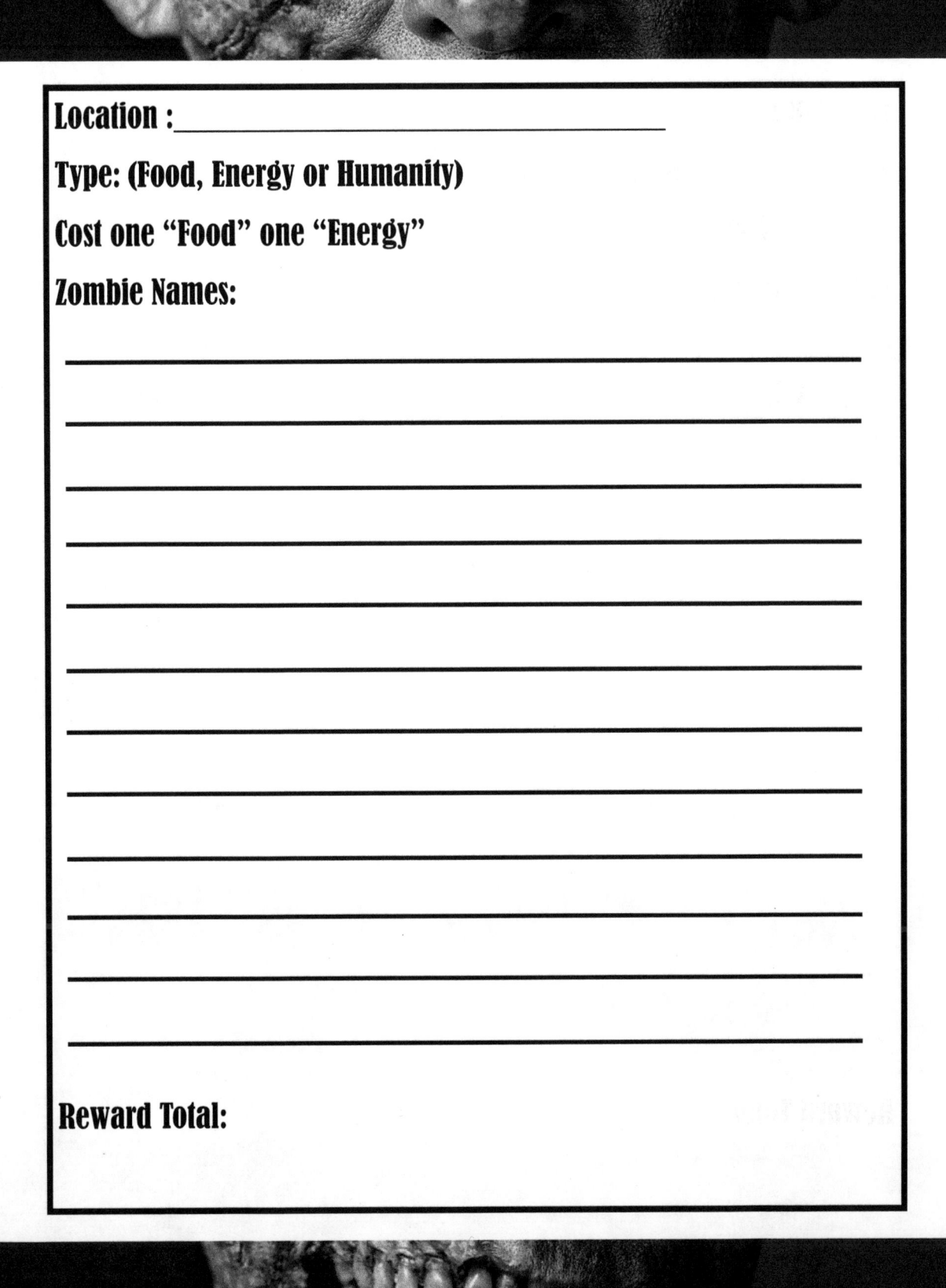

Location :_____

Type: (Food, Energy or Humanity)

Cost one "Food" one "Energy"

Zombie Names:

_____
_____
_____
_____
_____
_____
_____
_____
_____
_____
_____

Reward Total:

Location : _____

Type: (Food, Energy or Humanity)

Cost one "Food" one "Energy"

Zombie Names:

_____

_____

_____

_____

_____

_____

_____

_____

_____

_____

_____

_____

Reward Total:

Location : _____

Type: (Food, Energy or Humanity)

Cost one "Food" one "Energy"

Zombie Names:

_____
_____
_____
_____
_____
_____
_____
_____
_____
_____
_____
_____

Reward Total:

Location : _____

Type: (Food, Energy or Humanity)

Cost one "Food" one "Energy"

Zombie Names:

_____

_____

_____

_____

_____

_____

_____

_____

_____

_____

_____

Reward Total:

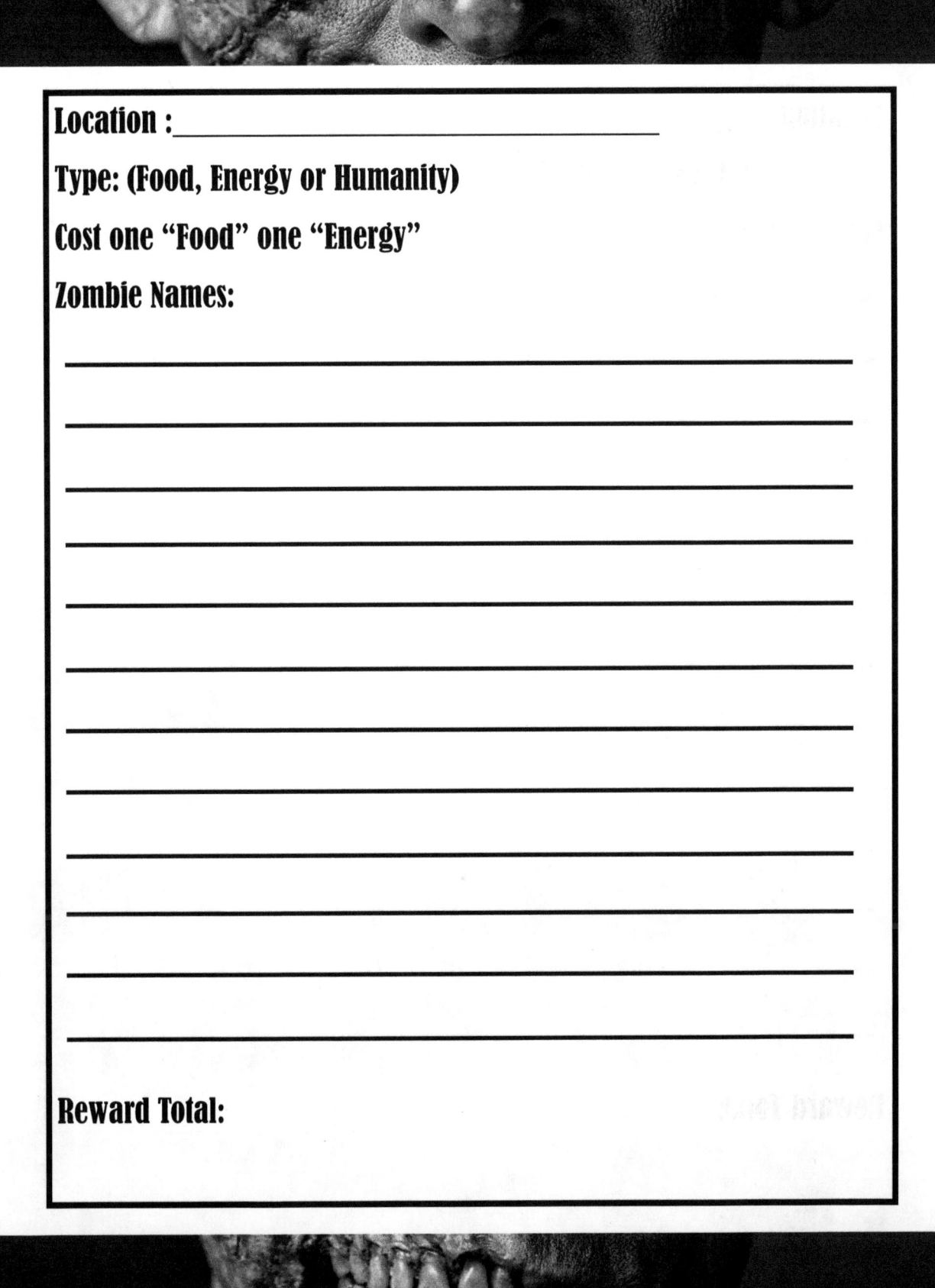

Location :_____

Type: (Food, Energy or Humanity)

Cost one "Food" one "Energy"

Zombie Names:

_____

_____

_____

_____

_____

_____

_____

_____

_____

_____

Reward Total:

Location : _____

Type: (Food, Energy or Humanity)

Cost one "Food" one "Energy"

Zombie Names:

_____

_____

_____

_____

_____

_____

_____

_____

_____

_____

_____

Reward Total:

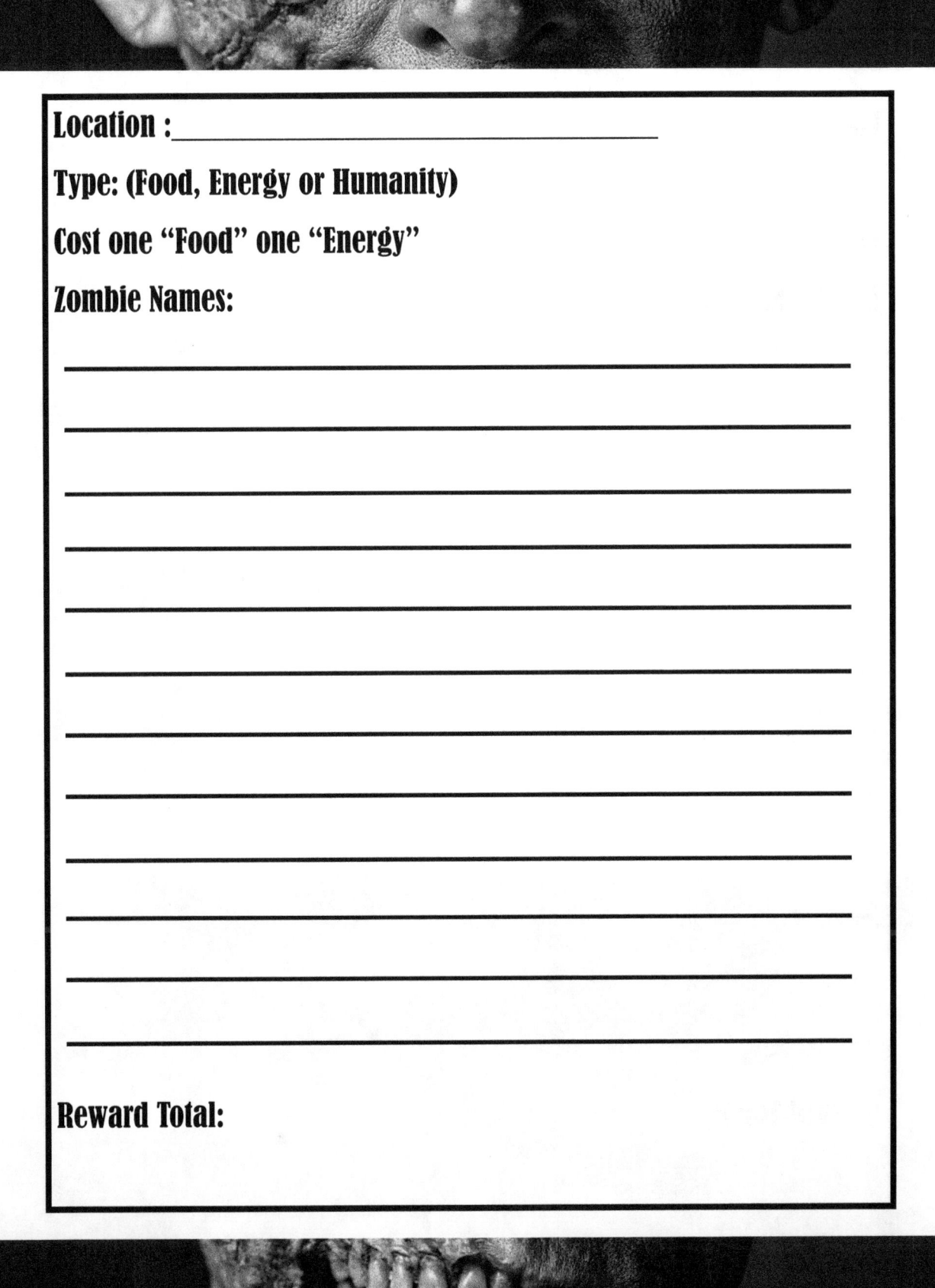

Location : _____

Type: (Food, Energy or Humanity)

Cost one "Food" one "Energy"

Zombie Names:

_____
_____
_____
_____
_____
_____
_____
_____
_____
_____
_____

Reward Total:

Location : _____

Type: (Food, Energy or Humanity)

Cost one "Food" one "Energy"

Zombie Names:

_____

_____

_____

_____

_____

_____

_____

_____

_____

_____

_____

Reward Total:

Location :_____

Type: (Food, Energy or Humanity)

Cost one "Food" one "Energy"

Zombie Names:

_____

_____

_____

_____

_____

_____

_____

_____

_____

_____

Reward Total:

Location : _____

Type: (Food, Energy or Humanity)

Cost one "Food" one "Energy"

Zombie Names:

_____

_____

_____

_____

_____

_____

_____

_____

_____

_____

Reward Total:

Location : _____

Type: (Food, Energy or Humanity)

Cost one "Food" one "Energy"

Zombie Names:

_____
_____
_____
_____
_____
_____
_____
_____
_____
_____

Reward Total:

Location : _____

Type: (Food, Energy or Humanity)

Cost one "Food" one "Energy"

Zombie Names:

_____

_____

_____

_____

_____

_____

_____

_____

_____

_____

_____

Reward Total:

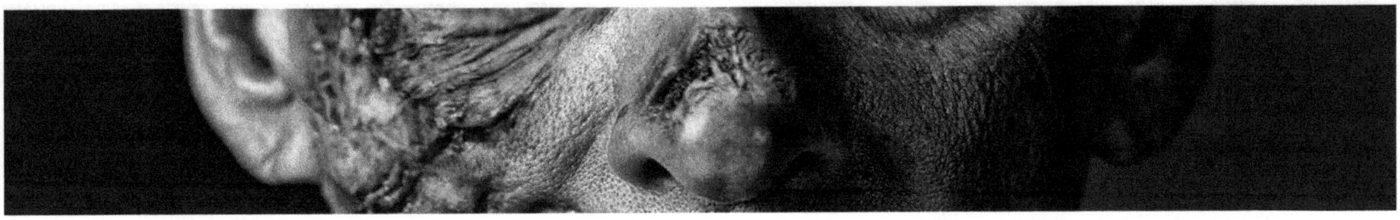

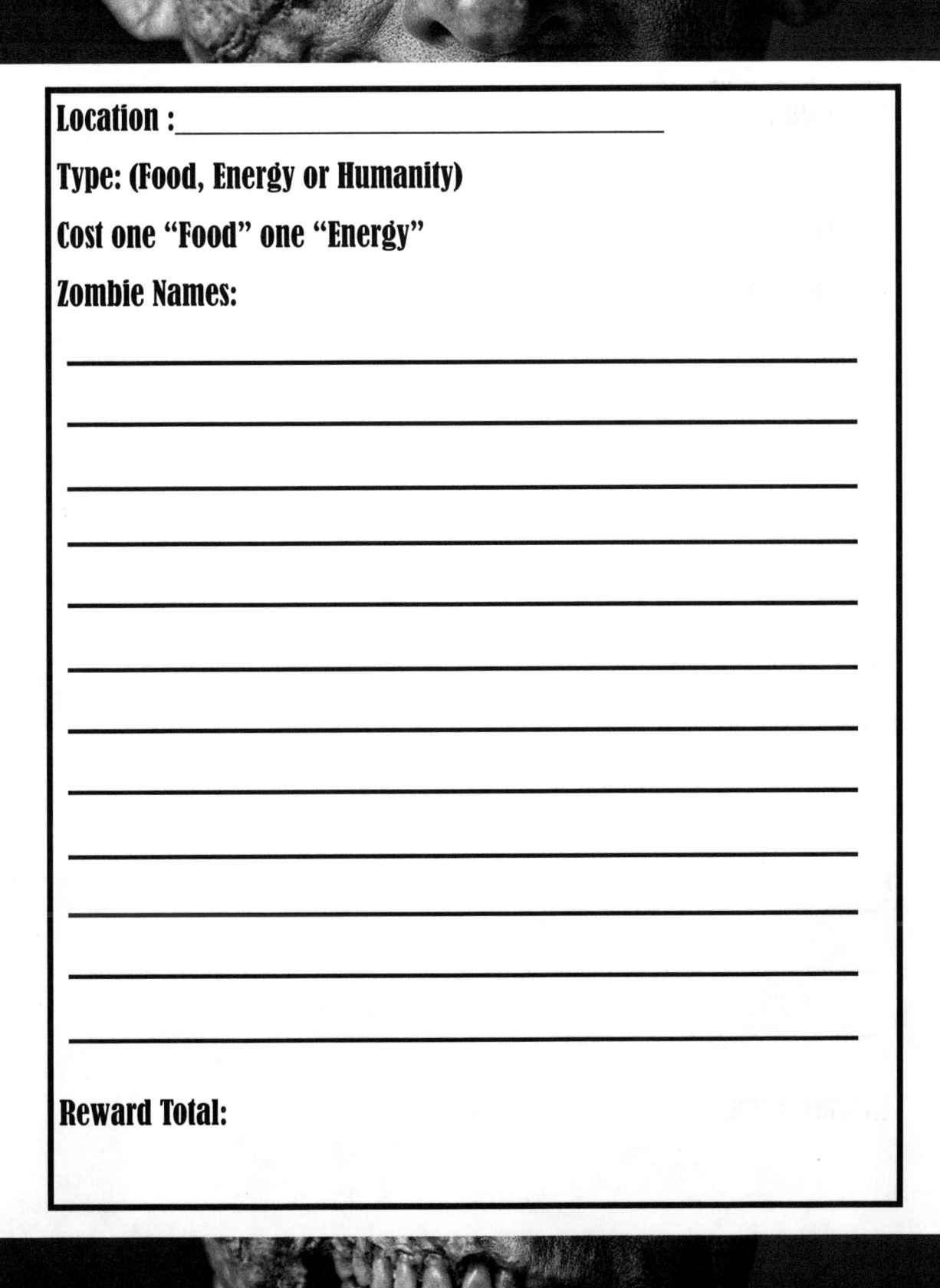

Location : _____

Type: (Food, Energy or Humanity)

Cost one "Food" one "Energy"

Zombie Names:

_____
_____
_____
_____
_____
_____
_____
_____
_____
_____
_____

Reward Total:

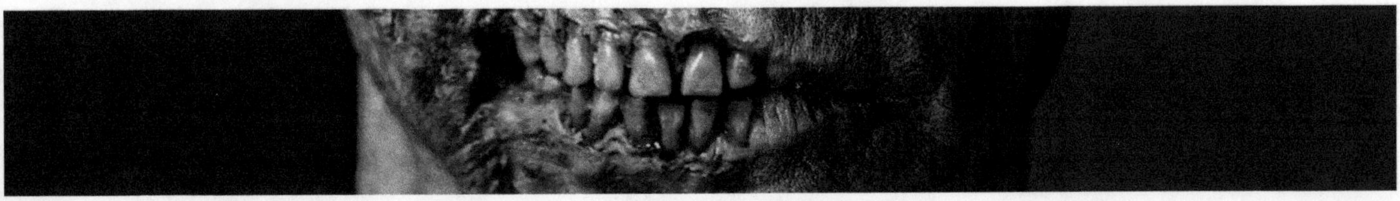

Location : _____

Type: (Food, Energy or Humanity)

Cost one "Food" one "Energy"

Zombie Names:

_____
_____
_____
_____
_____
_____
_____
_____
_____
_____
_____

Reward Total:

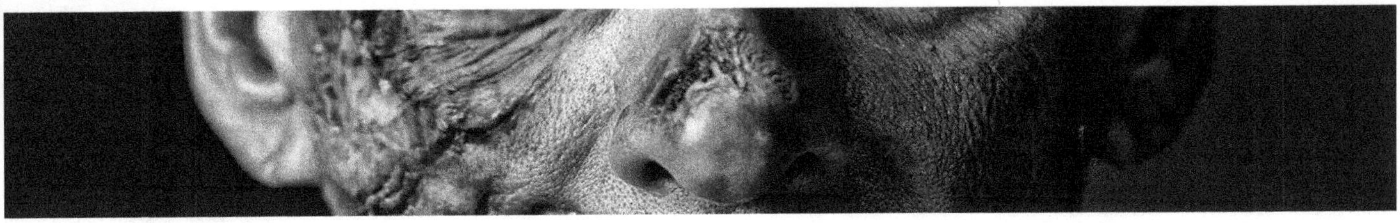

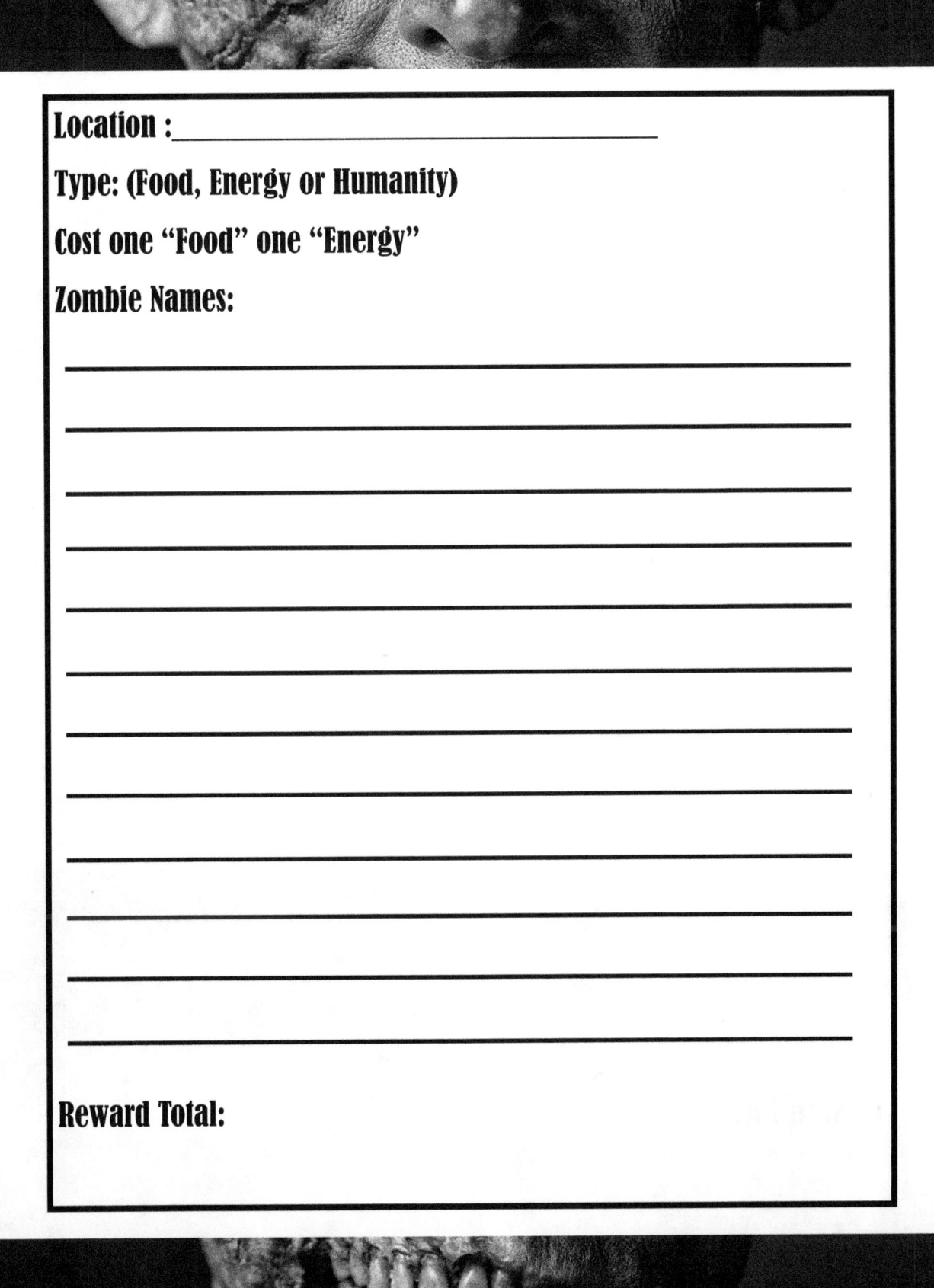

Location : _____

Type: (Food, Energy or Humanity)

Cost one "Food" one "Energy"

Zombie Names:

_____
_____
_____
_____
_____
_____
_____
_____
_____
_____
_____

Reward Total:

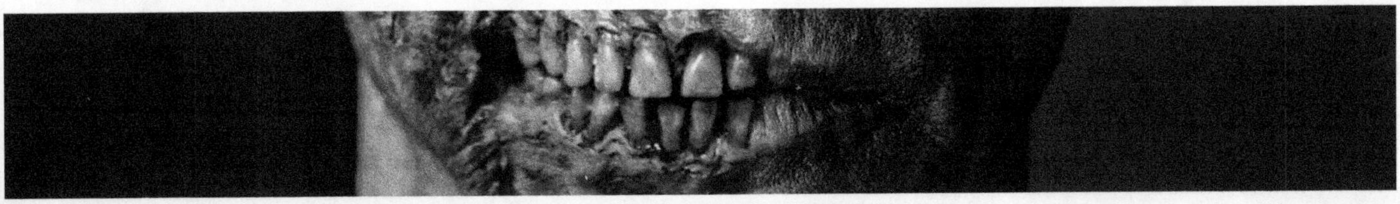

Location : _____

Type: (Food, Energy or Humanity)

Cost one "Food" one "Energy"

Zombie Names:

_____

_____

_____

_____

_____

_____

_____

_____

_____

_____

Reward Total:

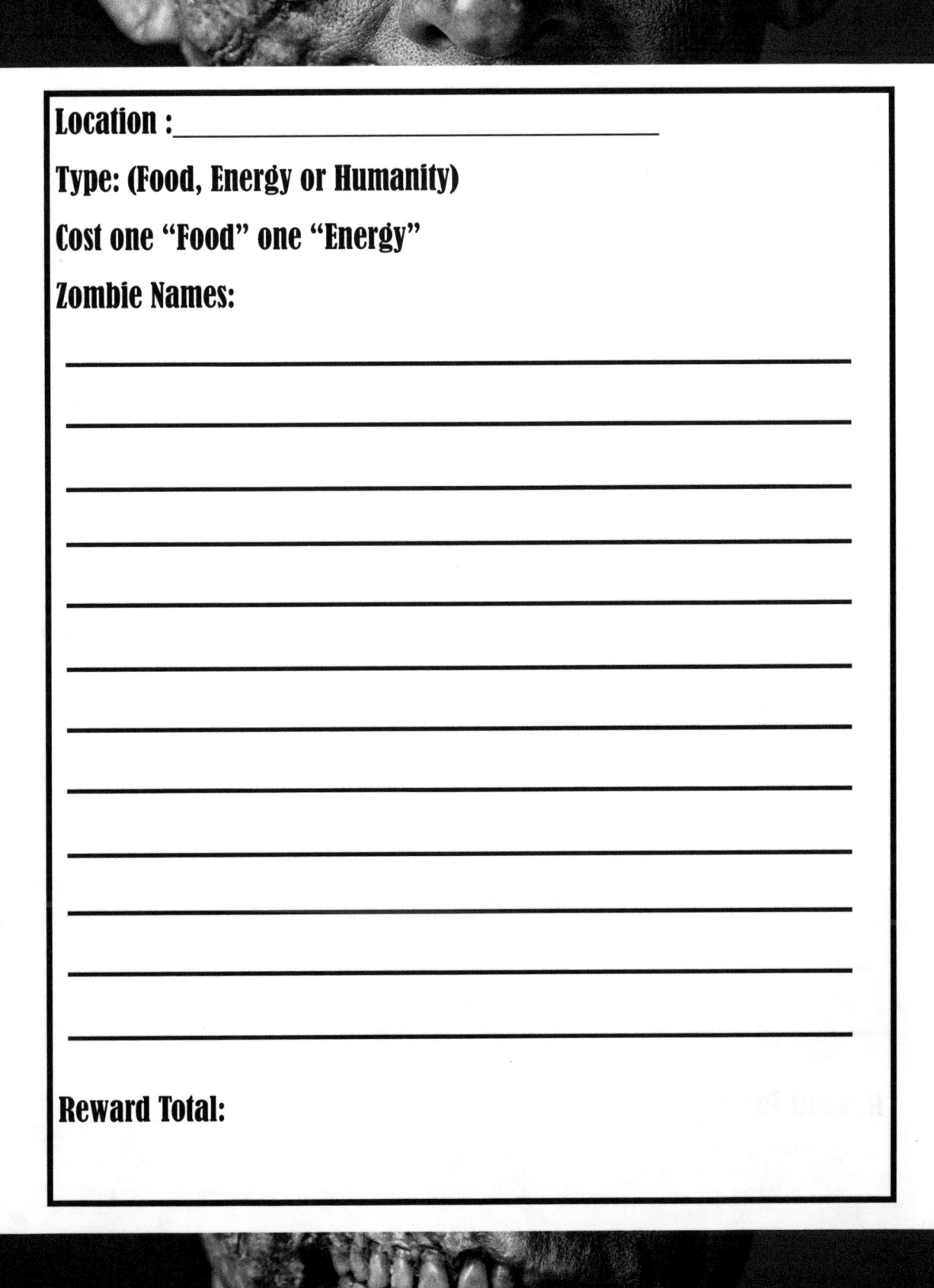

Location :_____

Type: (Food, Energy or Humanity)

Cost one "Food" one "Energy"

Zombie Names:

_____
_____
_____
_____
_____
_____
_____
_____
_____
_____
_____

Reward Total:

Location :_____

Type: (Food, Energy or Humanity)

Cost one "Food" one "Energy"

Zombie Names:

_____
_____
_____
_____
_____
_____
_____
_____
_____
_____

Reward Total:

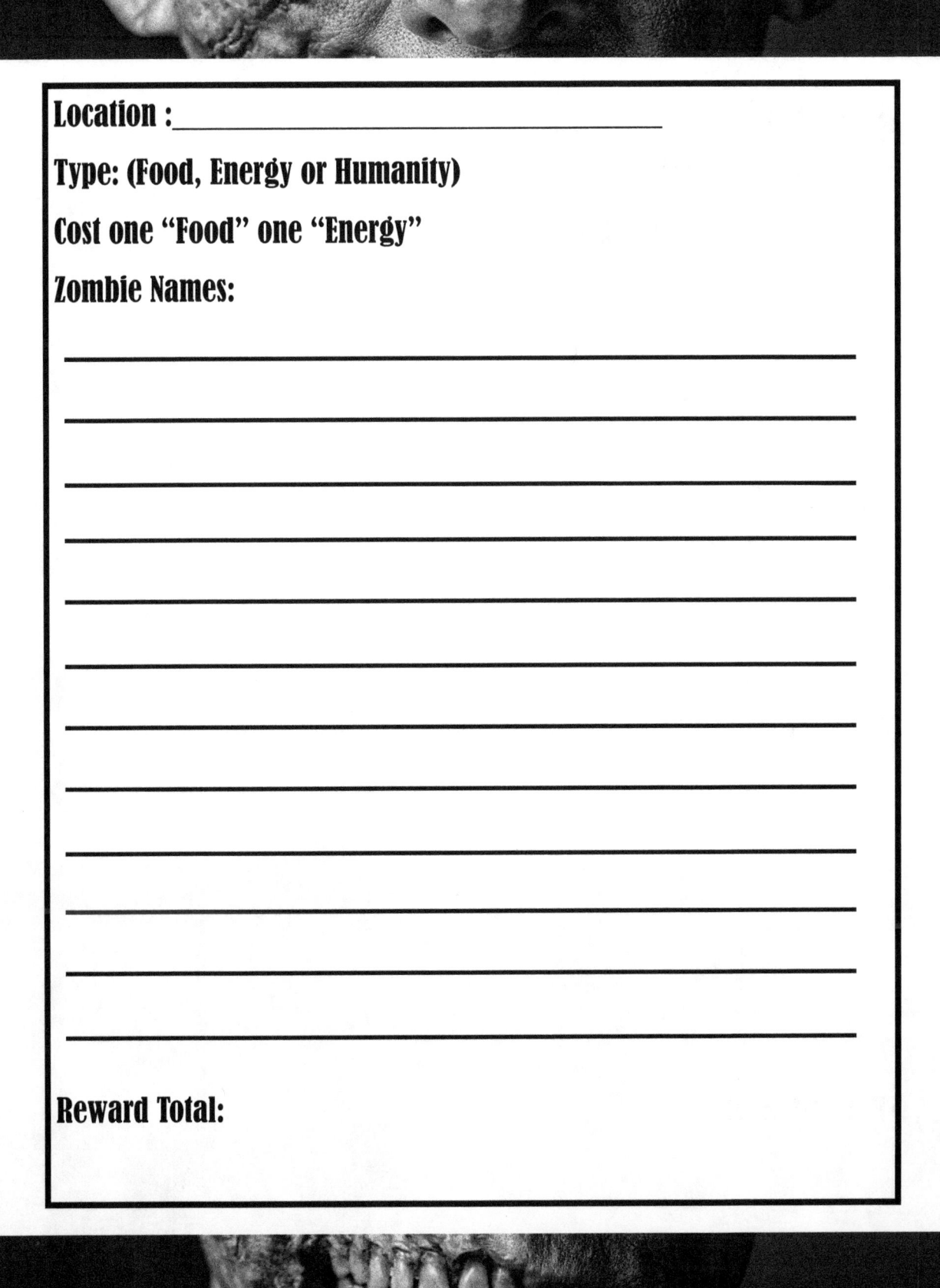

Location :_____

Type: (Food, Energy or Humanity)

Cost one "Food" one "Energy"

Zombie Names:

_____
_____
_____
_____
_____
_____
_____
_____
_____
_____

Reward Total:

Location : _____

Type: (Food, Energy or Humanity)

Cost one "Food" one "Energy"

Zombie Names:

_____
_____
_____
_____
_____
_____
_____
_____
_____
_____
_____
_____

Reward Total:

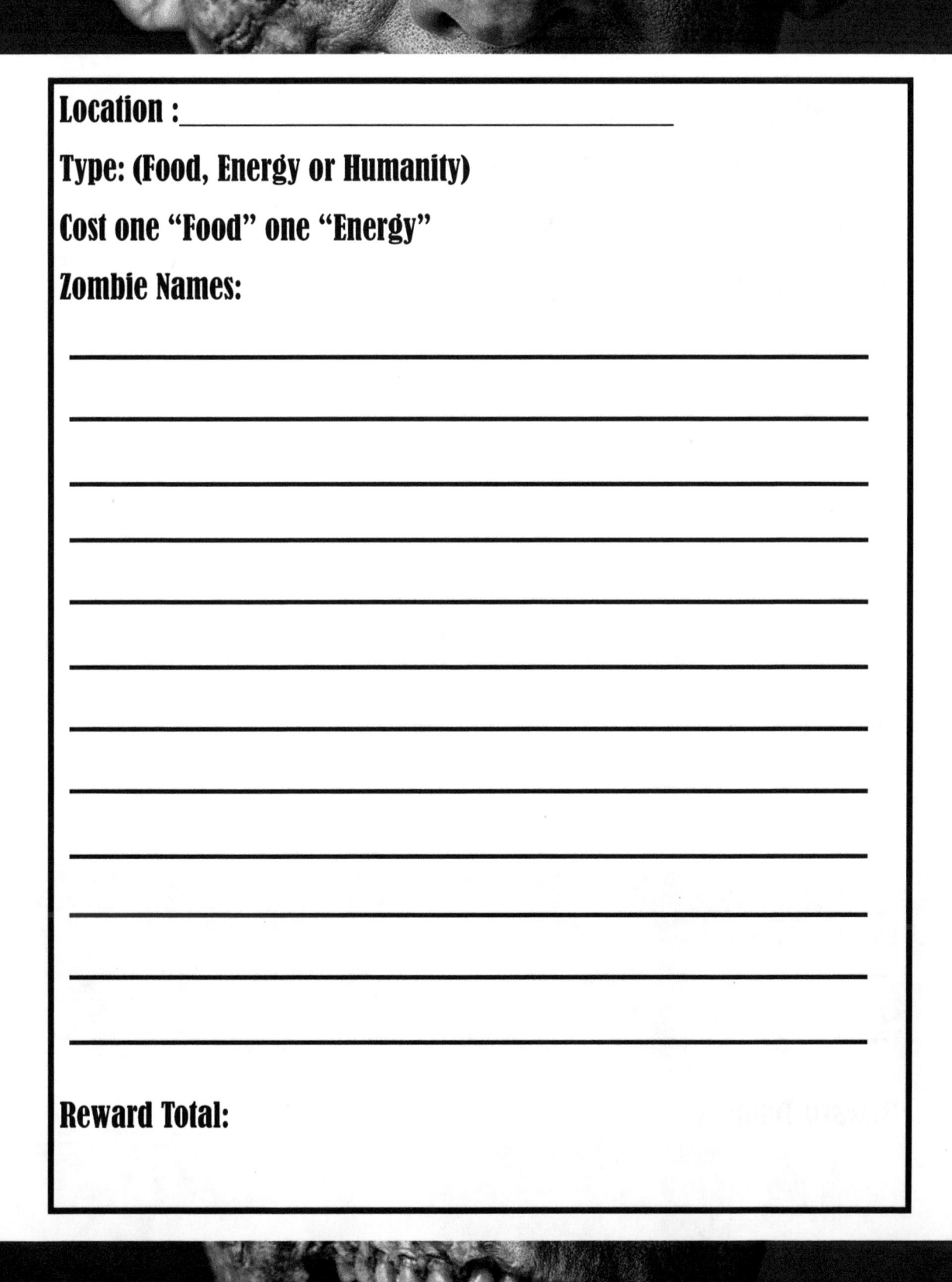

Location :_____

Type: (Food, Energy or Humanity)

Cost one "Food" one "Energy"

Zombie Names:

_____

_____

_____

_____

_____

_____

_____

_____

_____

_____

Reward Total:

Location : _____

Type: (Food, Energy or Humanity)

Cost one "Food" one "Energy"

Zombie Names:

_____
_____
_____
_____
_____
_____
_____
_____
_____
_____
_____

Reward Total:

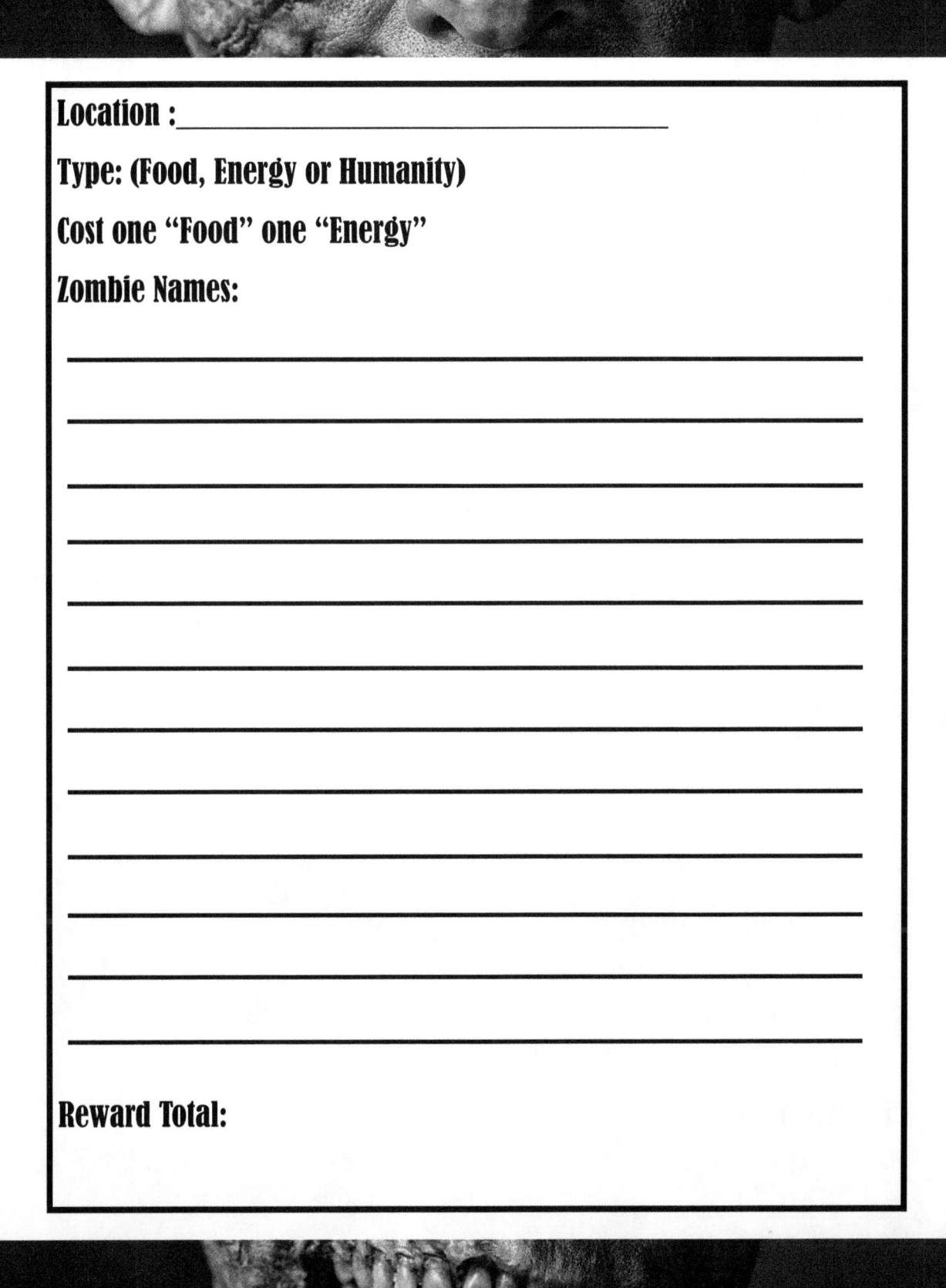

Location : _____

Type: (Food, Energy or Humanity)

Cost one "Food" one "Energy"

Zombie Names:

_____

_____

_____

_____

_____

_____

_____

_____

_____

_____

Reward Total:

Location : _____

Type: (Food, Energy or Humanity)

Cost one "Food" one "Energy"

Zombie Names:

_____
_____
_____
_____
_____
_____
_____
_____
_____
_____
_____

Reward Total:

Location :_____

Type: (Food, Energy or Humanity)

Cost one "Food" one "Energy"

Zombie Names:

_____
_____
_____
_____
_____
_____
_____
_____
_____
_____
_____
_____

Reward Total:

Location :_____

Type: (Food, Energy or Humanity)

Cost one "Food" one "Energy"

Zombie Names:

_____
_____
_____
_____
_____
_____
_____
_____
_____
_____
_____

Reward Total:

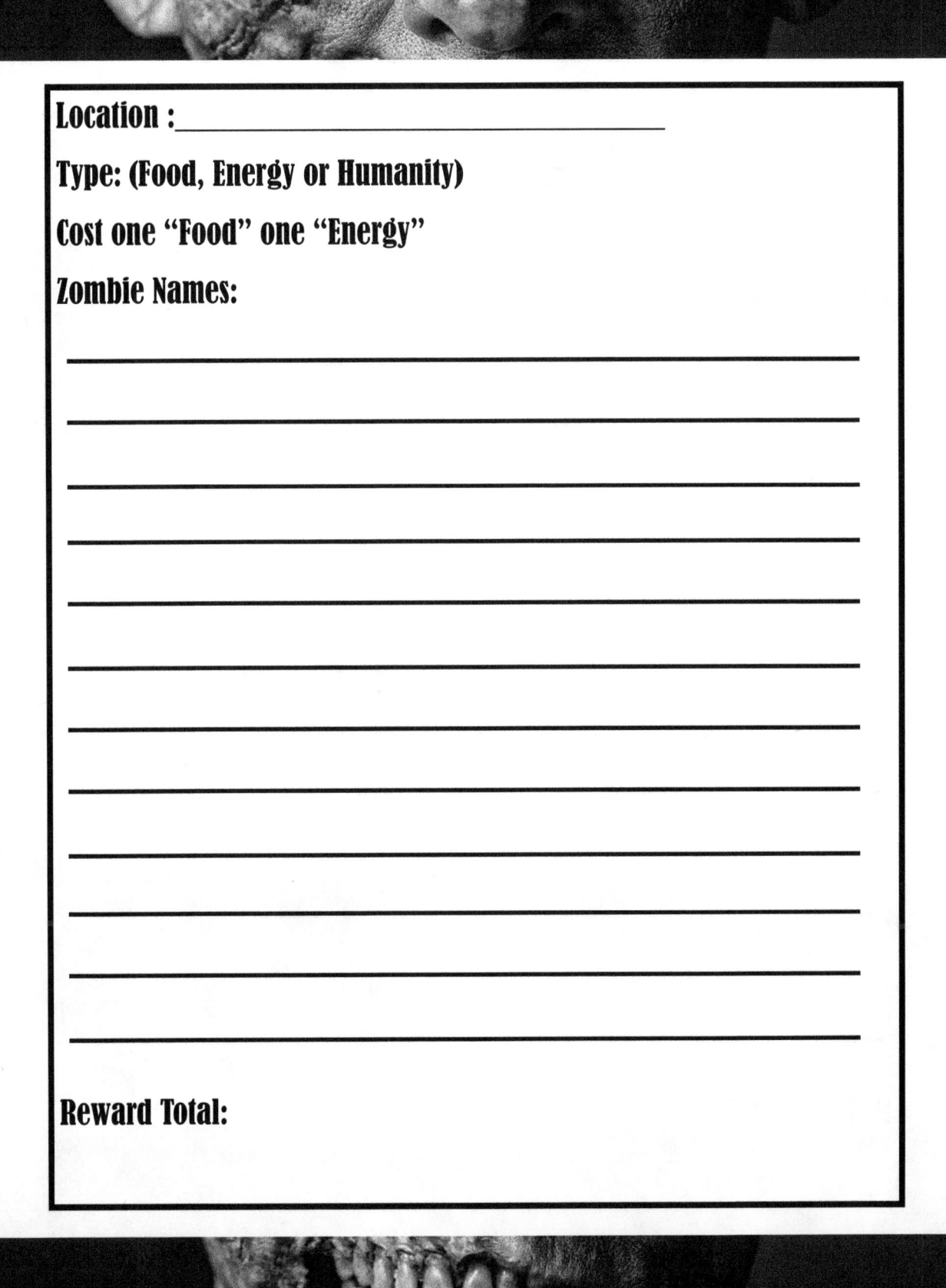

Location : _____

Type: (Food, Energy or Humanity)

Cost one "Food" one "Energy"

Zombie Names:

_____
_____
_____
_____
_____
_____
_____
_____
_____
_____
_____

Reward Total:

Location :_____

Type: (Food, Energy or Humanity)

Cost one "Food" one "Energy"

Zombie Names:

_____

_____

_____

_____

_____

_____

_____

_____

_____

_____

Reward Total:

Location : _____

Type: (Food, Energy or Humanity)

Cost one "Food" one "Energy"

Zombie Names:

_____

_____

_____

_____

_____

_____

_____

_____

_____

_____

Reward Total:

Location :_____

Type: (Food, Energy or Humanity)

Cost one "Food" one "Energy"

Zombie Names:

_____
_____
_____
_____
_____
_____
_____
_____
_____
_____
_____
_____

Reward Total:

Location : _____

Type: (Food, Energy or Humanity)

Cost one "Food" one "Energy"

Zombie Names:

_____
_____
_____
_____
_____
_____
_____
_____
_____
_____
_____

Reward Total:

Location : _____

Type: (Food, Energy or Humanity)

Cost one "Food" one "Energy"

Zombie Names:

_____

_____

_____

_____

_____

_____

_____

_____

_____

_____

_____

Reward Total:

Location : _____

Type: (Food, Energy or Humanity)

Cost one "Food" one "Energy"

Zombie Names:

_____

_____

_____

_____

_____

_____

_____

_____

_____

_____

_____

Reward Total:

Location :_____

Type: (Food, Energy or Humanity)

Cost one "Food" one "Energy"

Zombie Names:

_____

_____

_____

_____

_____

_____

_____

_____

_____

_____

_____

Reward Total:

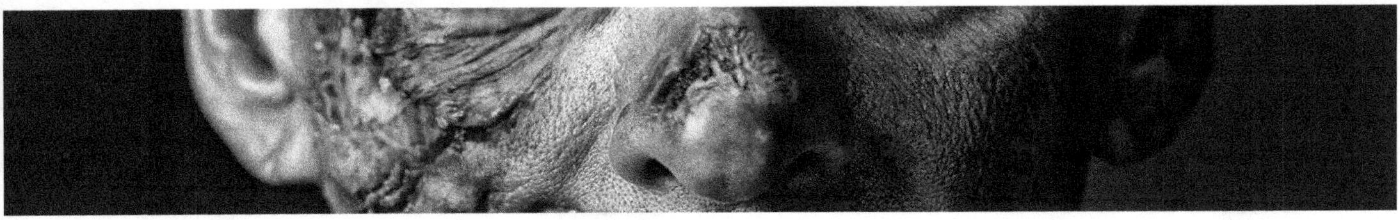

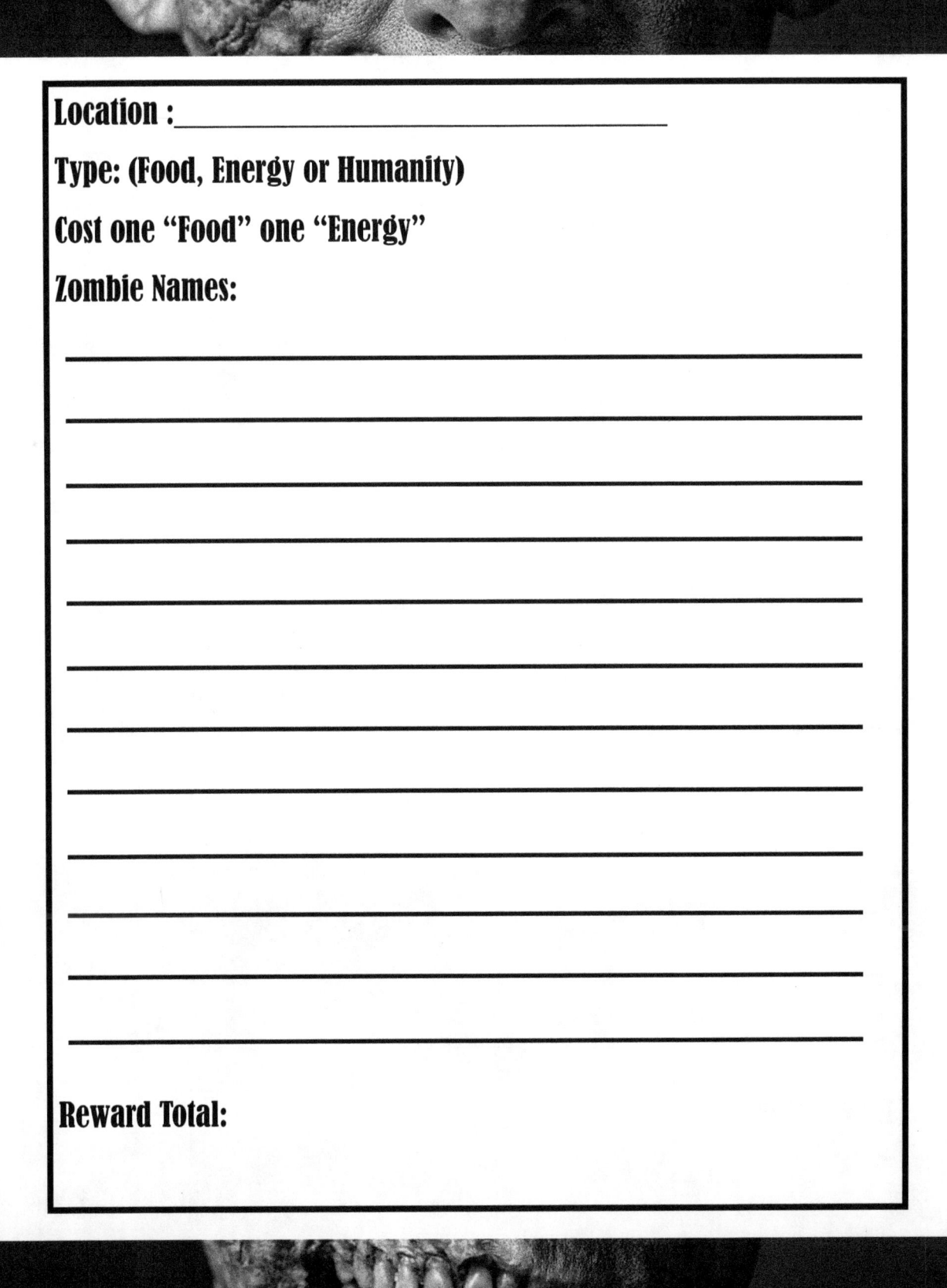

Location :_____

Type: (Food, Energy or Humanity)

Cost one "Food" one "Energy"

Zombie Names:

_____
_____
_____
_____
_____
_____
_____
_____
_____
_____
_____
_____

Reward Total:

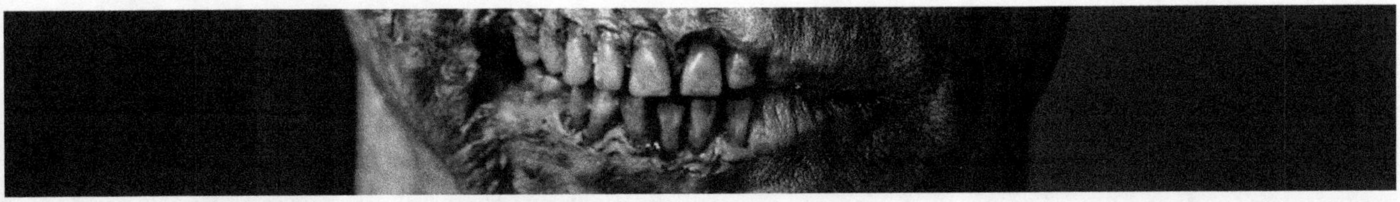

Location : _____

Type: (Food, Energy or Humanity)

Cost one "Food" one "Energy"

Zombie Names:

_____

_____

_____

_____

_____

_____

_____

_____

_____

_____

_____

_____

Reward Total:

Location : _____

Type: (Food, Energy or Humanity)

Cost one "Food" one "Energy"

Zombie Names:

_____
_____
_____
_____
_____
_____
_____
_____
_____
_____
_____
_____

Reward Total:

Location :_____

Type: (Food, Energy or Humanity)

Cost one "Food" one "Energy"

Zombie Names:

_____

_____

_____

_____

_____

_____

_____

_____

_____

_____

Reward Total:

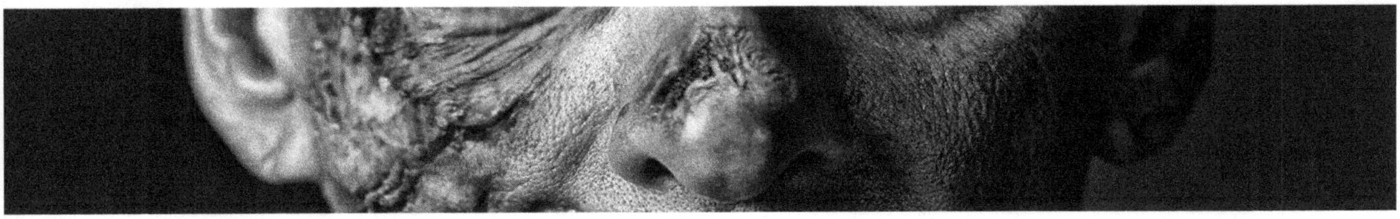

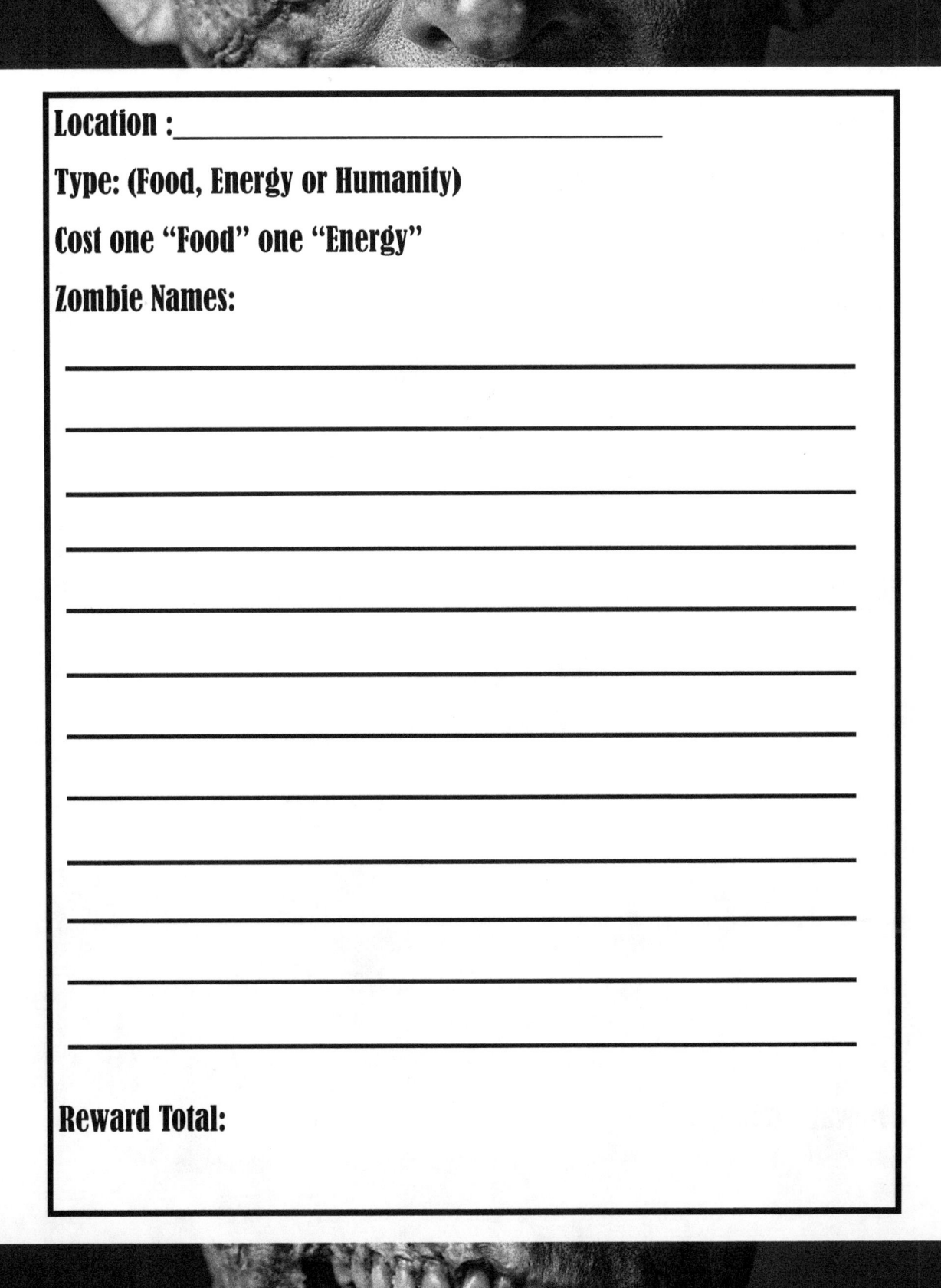

Location : _____

Type: (Food, Energy or Humanity)

Cost one "Food" one "Energy"

Zombie Names:

_____

_____

_____

_____

_____

_____

_____

_____

_____

_____

Reward Total:

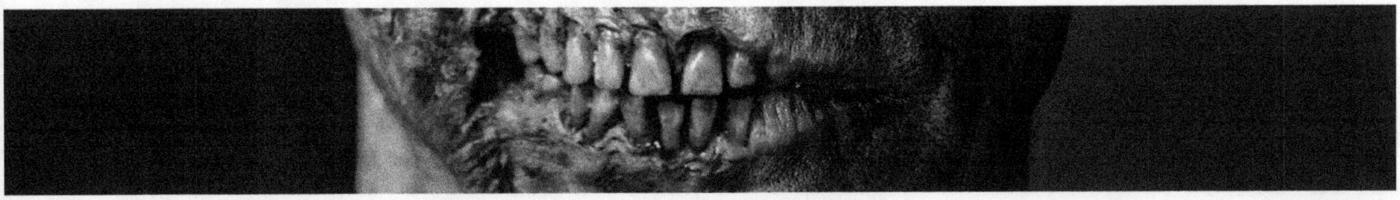

Location : _____

Type: (Food, Energy or Humanity)

Cost one "Food" one "Energy"

Zombie Names:

_____

_____

_____

_____

_____

_____

_____

_____

_____

_____

_____

Reward Total:

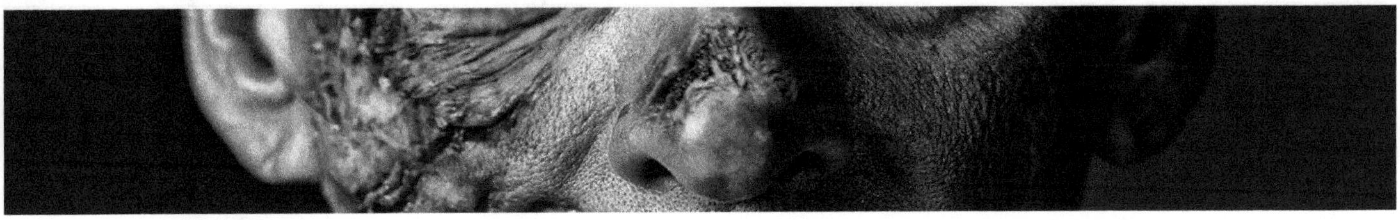

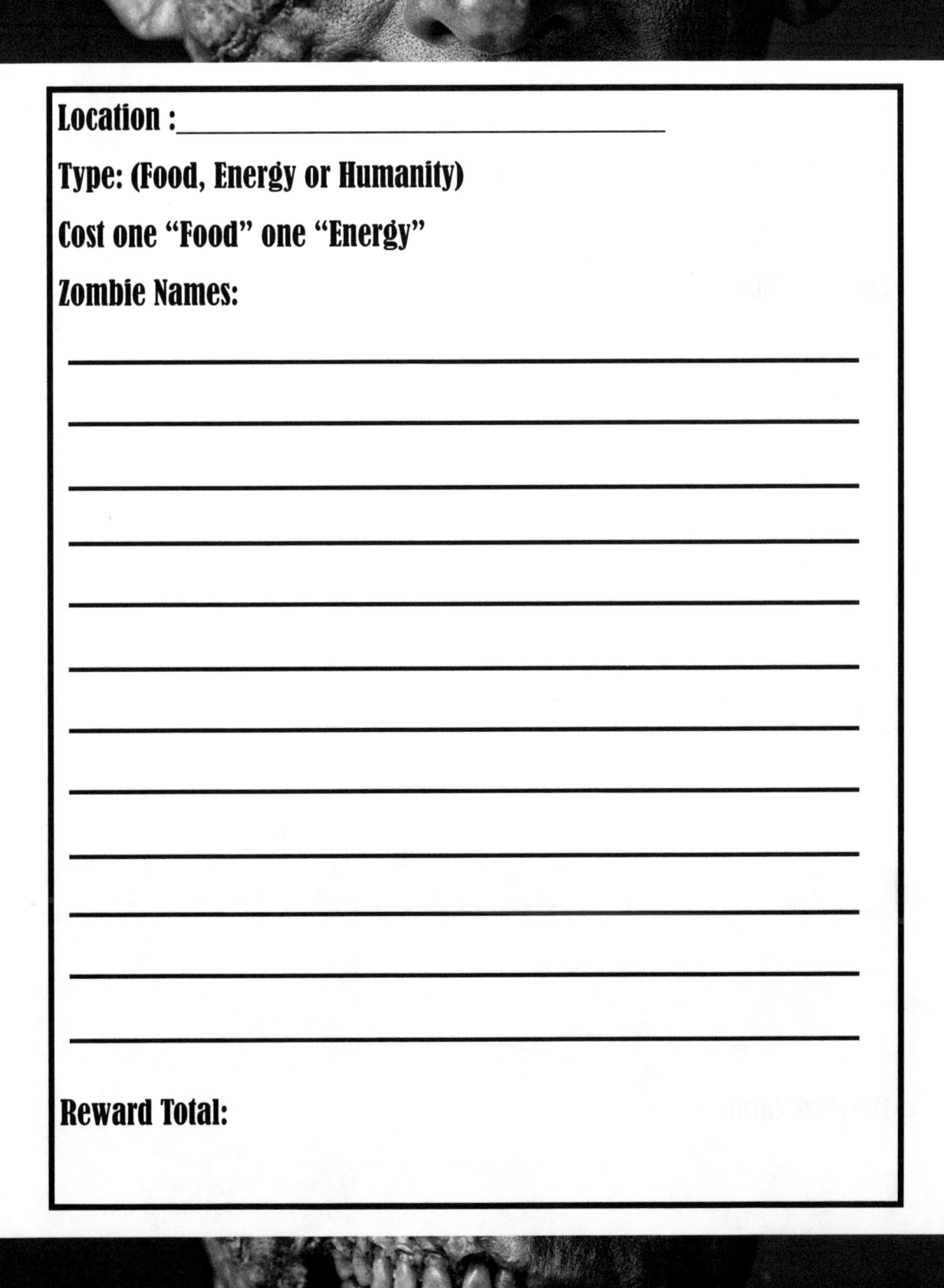

Location : _____

Type: (Food, Energy or Humanity)

Cost one "Food" one "Energy"

Zombie Names:

_____

_____

_____

_____

_____

_____

_____

_____

_____

_____

_____

Reward Total:

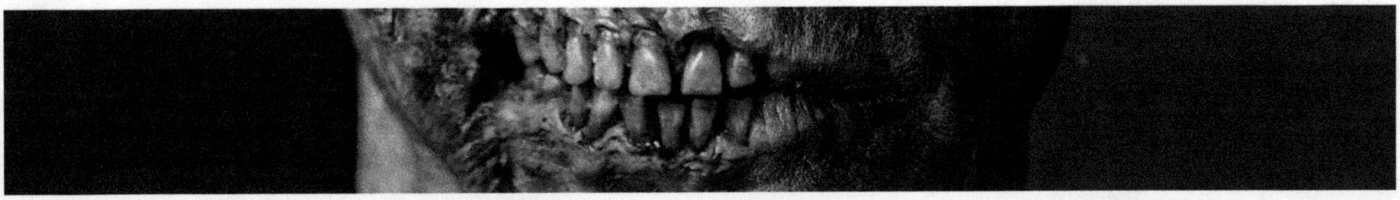

Location :_____

Type: (Food, Energy or Humanity)

Cost one "Food" one "Energy"

Zombie Names:

_____
_____
_____
_____
_____
_____
_____
_____
_____
_____
_____

Reward Total:

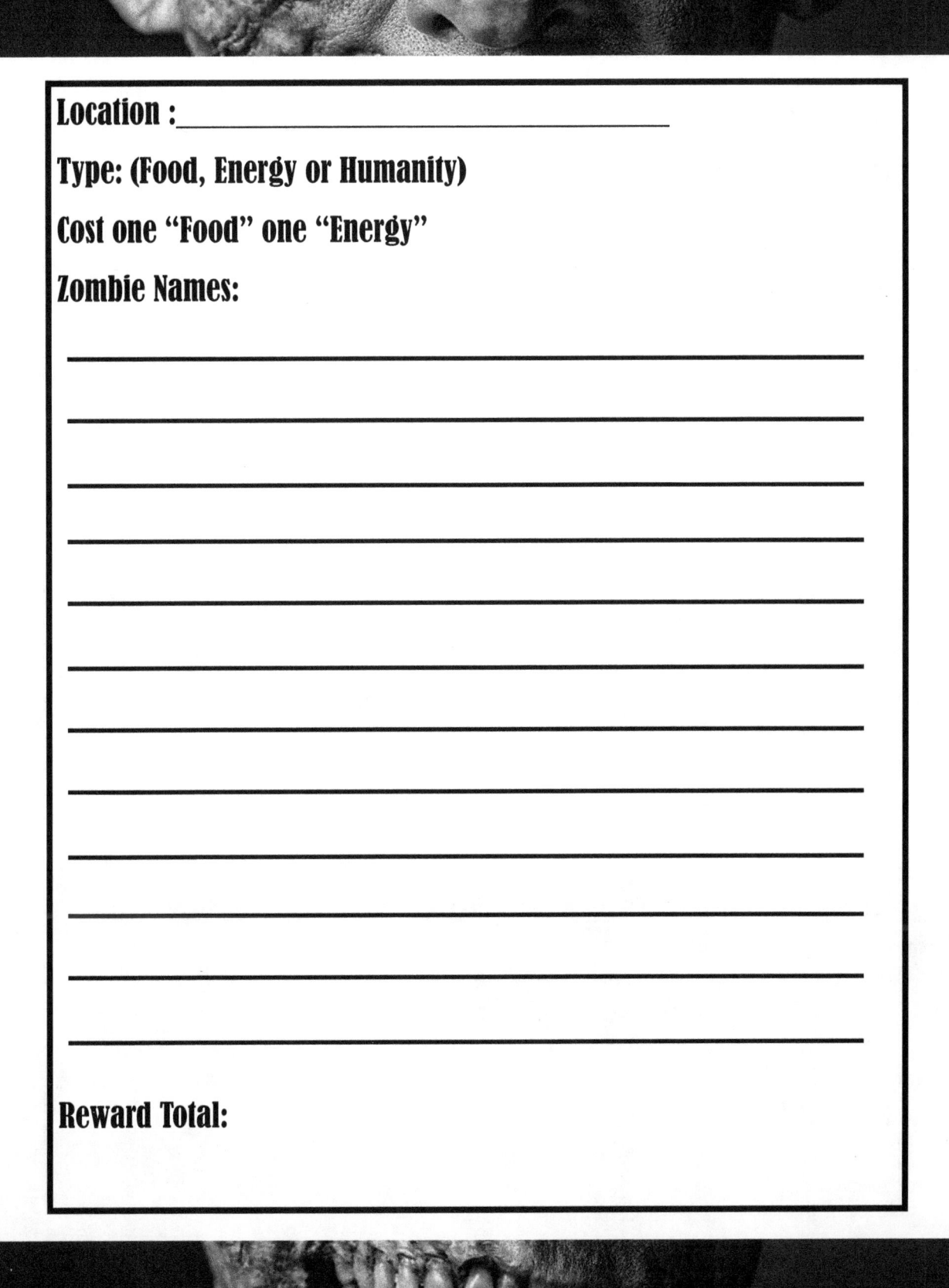

Location : _____

Type: (Food, Energy or Humanity)

Cost one "Food" one "Energy"

Zombie Names:

_____
_____
_____
_____
_____
_____
_____
_____
_____
_____
_____
_____

Reward Total:

Location :_____

Type: (Food, Energy or Humanity)

Cost one "Food" one "Energy"

Zombie Names:

_____

_____

_____

_____

_____

_____

_____

_____

_____

_____

_____

Reward Total:

Location : _____

Type: (Food, Energy or Humanity)

Cost one "Food" one "Energy"

Zombie Names:

_____
_____
_____
_____
_____
_____
_____
_____
_____
_____
_____

Reward Total:

Location : _____

Type: (Food, Energy or Humanity)

Cost one "Food" one "Energy"

Zombie Names:

_____
_____
_____
_____
_____
_____
_____
_____
_____
_____
_____
_____

Reward Total:

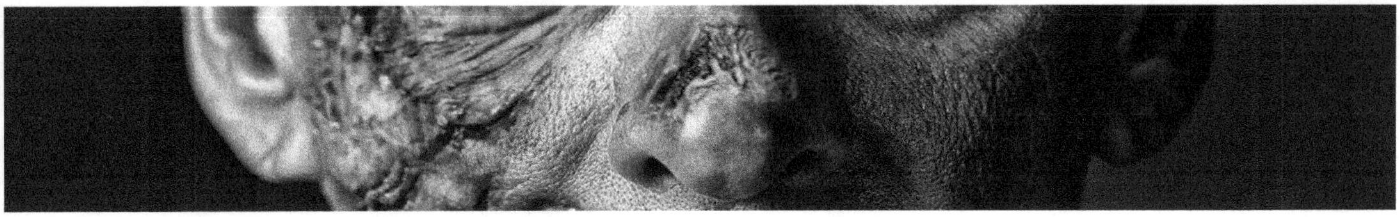

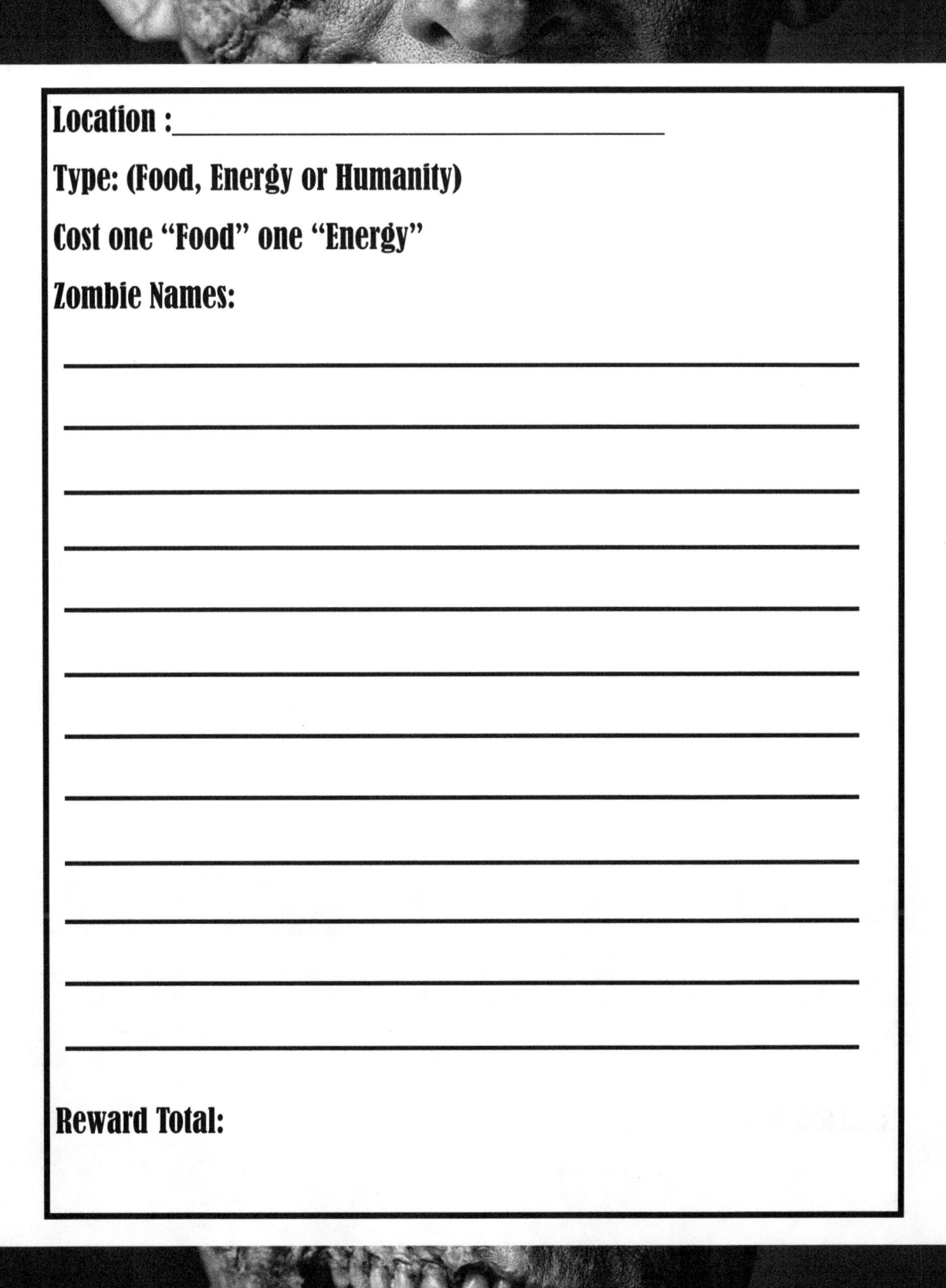

Location : _____

Type: (Food, Energy or Humanity)

Cost one "Food" one "Energy"

Zombie Names:

_____

_____

_____

_____

_____

_____

_____

_____

_____

_____

Reward Total:

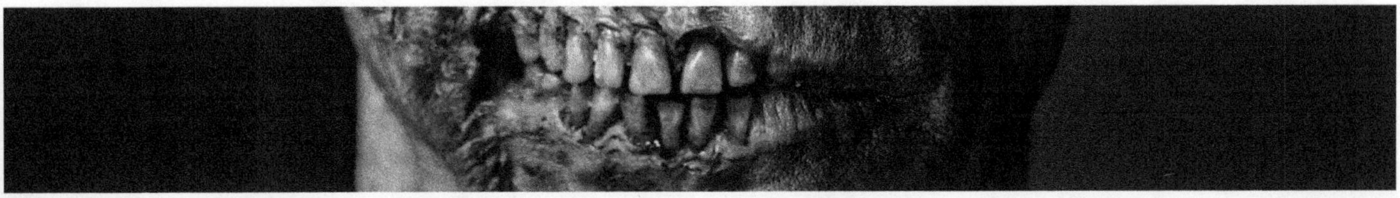

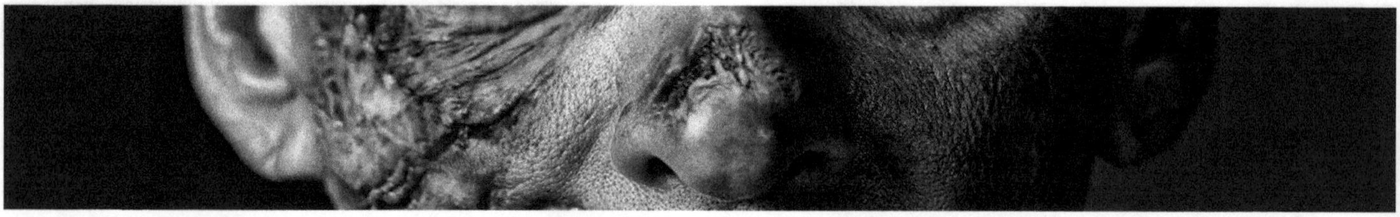

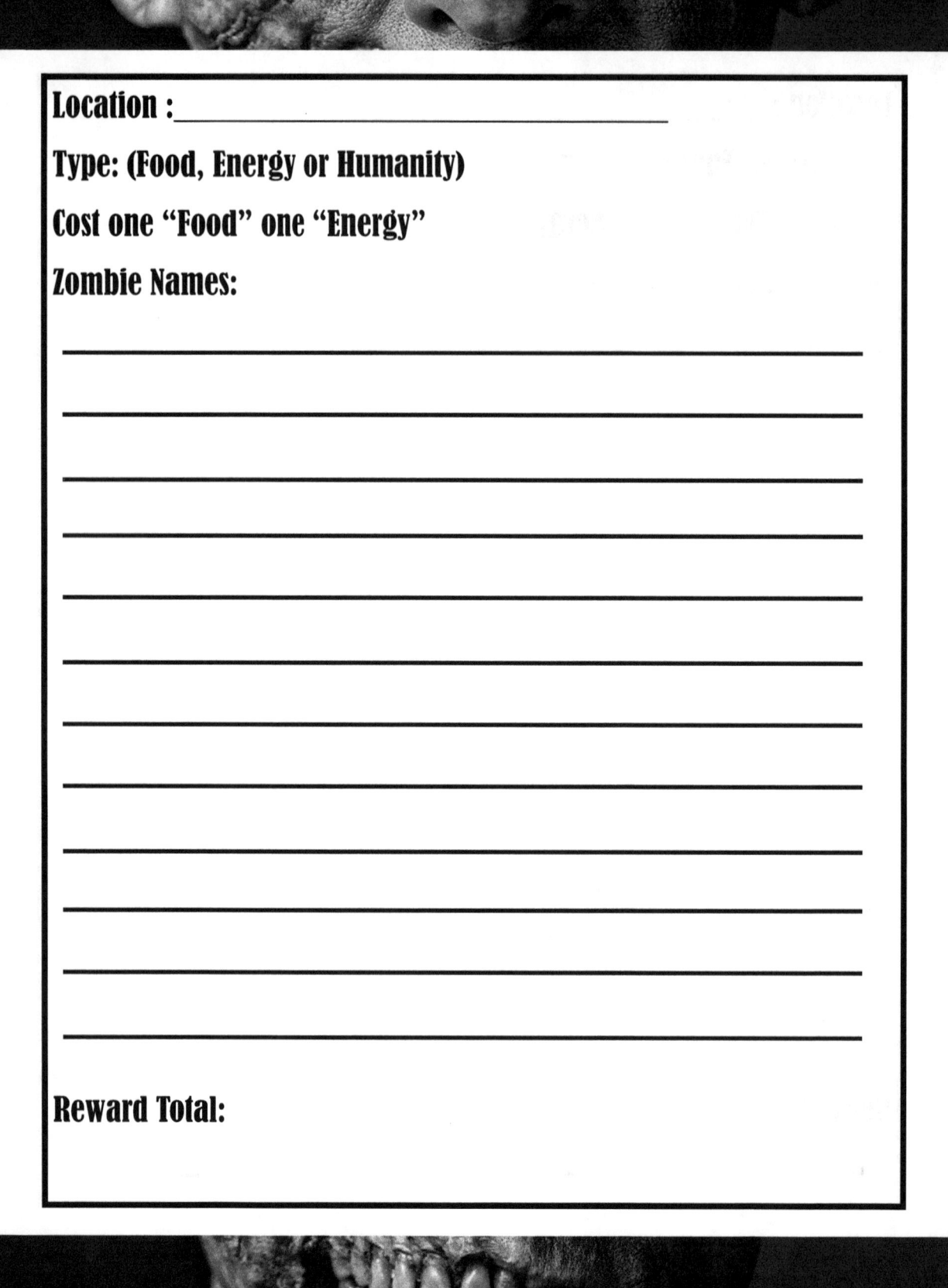

Location :_____

Type: (Food, Energy or Humanity)

Cost one "Food" one "Energy"

Zombie Names:

_____

_____

_____

_____

_____

_____

_____

_____

_____

_____

_____

Reward Total:

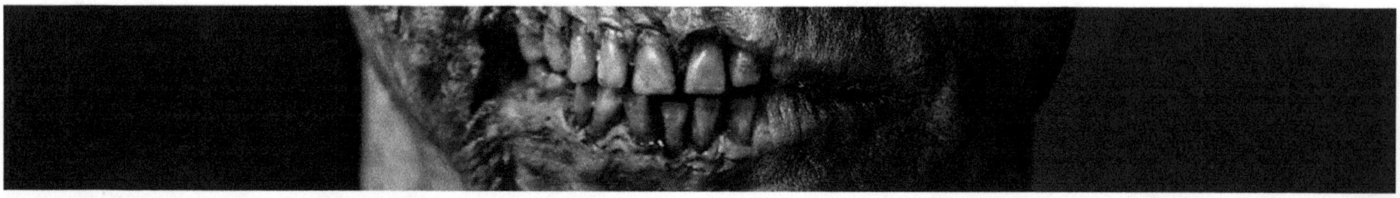

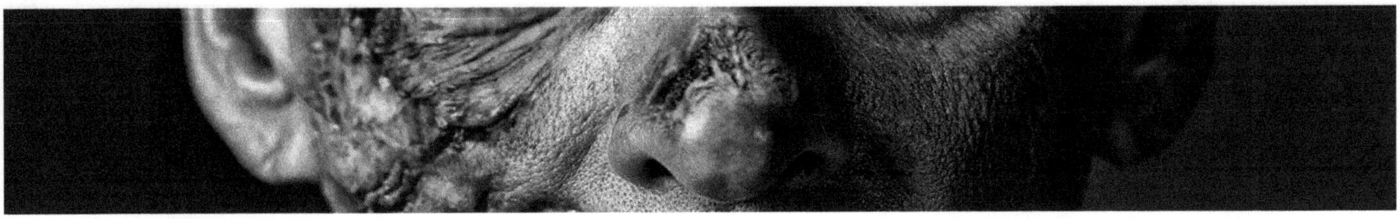

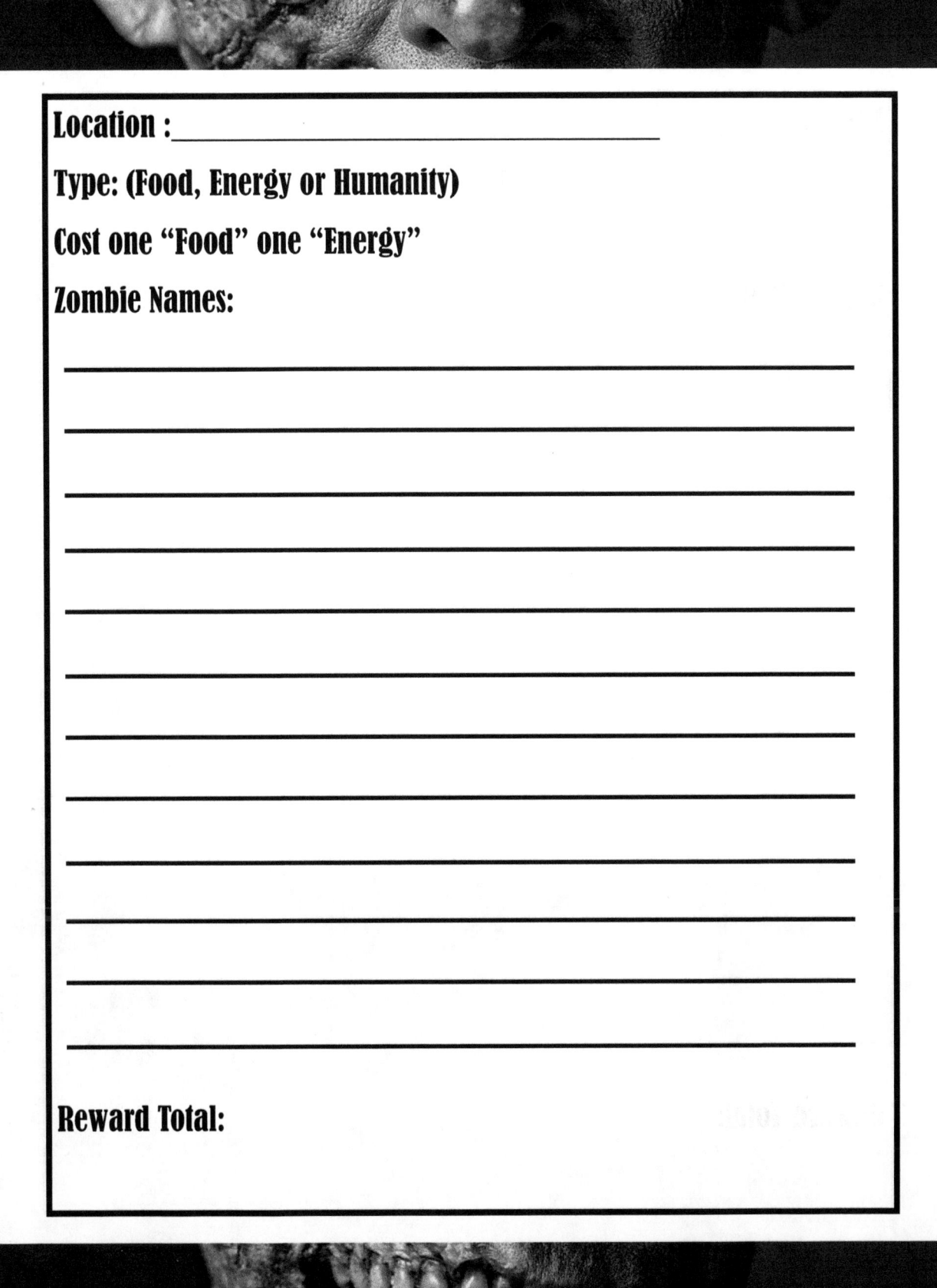

Location : _____

Type: (Food, Energy or Humanity)

Cost one "Food" one "Energy"

Zombie Names:

_____
_____
_____
_____
_____
_____
_____
_____
_____
_____

Reward Total:

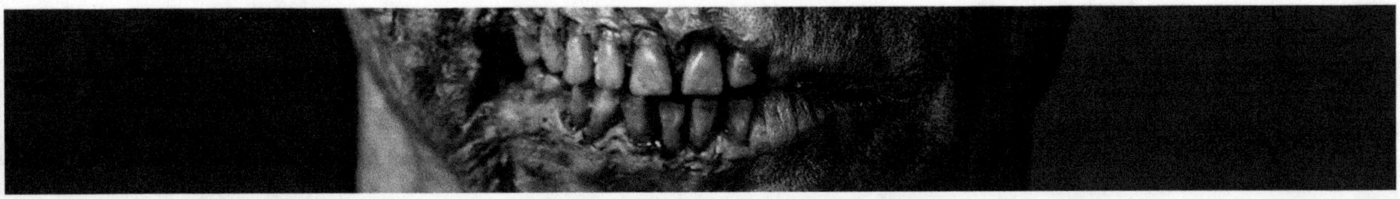

Location :_____

Type: (Food, Energy or Humanity)

Cost one "Food" one "Energy"

Zombie Names:

_____
_____
_____
_____
_____
_____
_____
_____
_____
_____
_____

Reward Total:

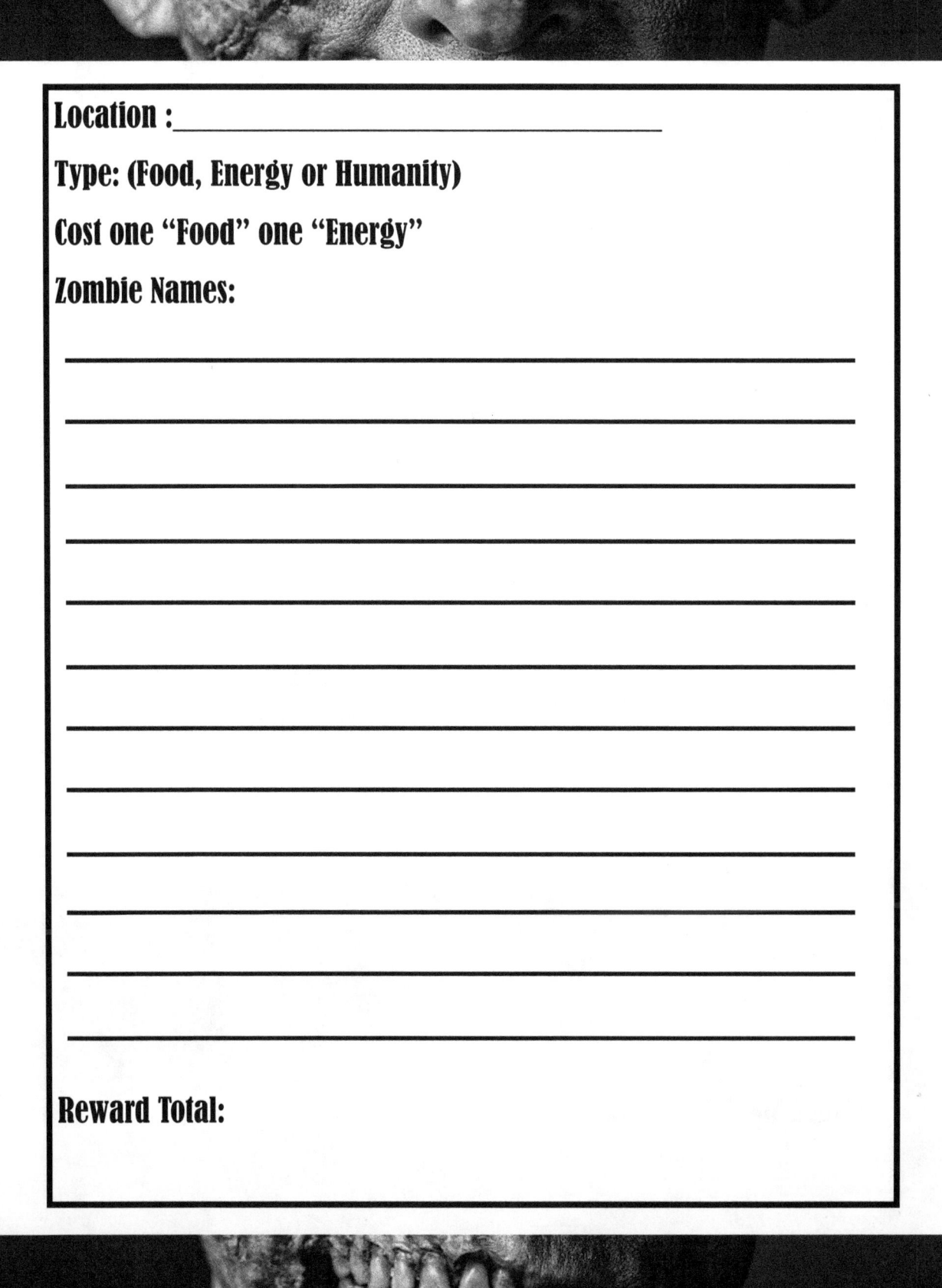

Location : _____

Type: (Food, Energy or Humanity)

Cost one "Food" one "Energy"

Zombie Names:

_____

_____

_____

_____

_____

_____

_____

_____

_____

_____

Reward Total:

Location : _____

Type: (Food, Energy or Humanity)

Cost one "Food" one "Energy"

Zombie Names:

_____

_____

_____

_____

_____

_____

_____

_____

_____

_____

Reward Total:

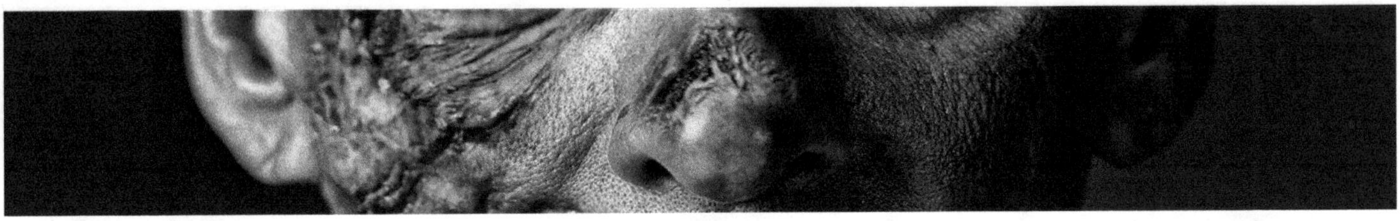

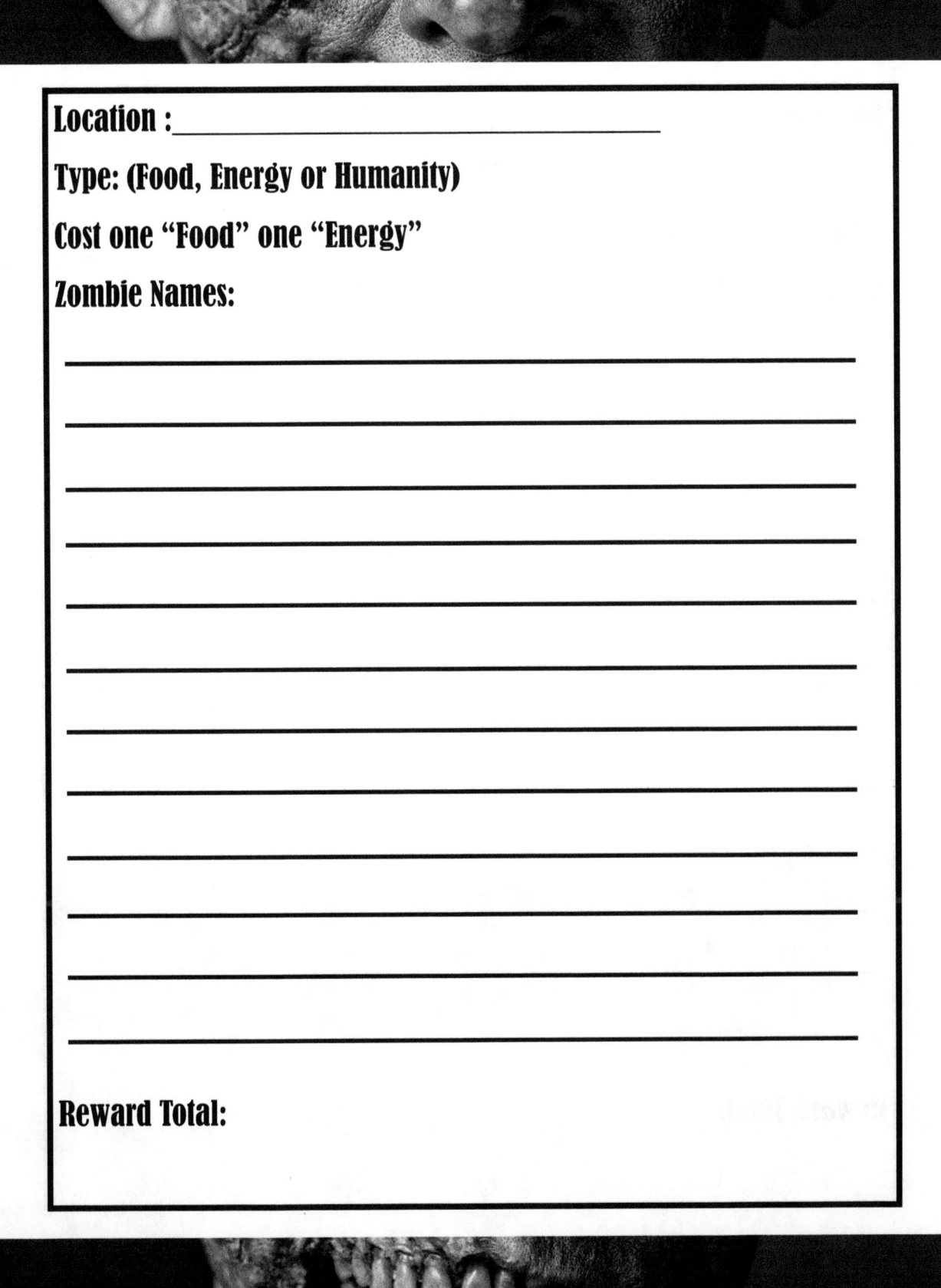

Location : _____

Type: (Food, Energy or Humanity)

Cost one "Food" one "Energy"

Zombie Names:

_____

_____

_____

_____

_____

_____

_____

_____

_____

_____

Reward Total:

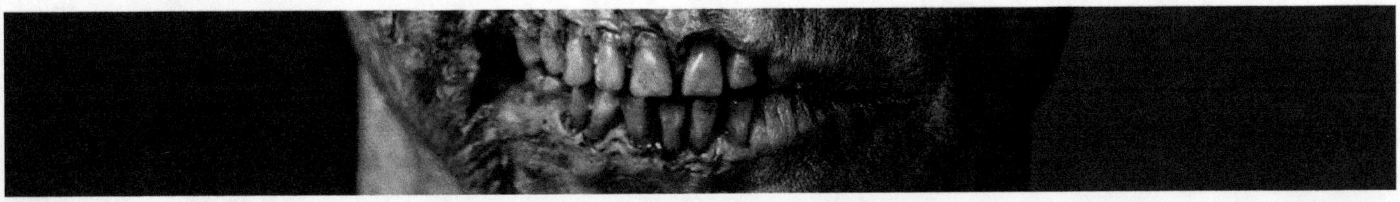

Location :_____

Type: (Food, Energy or Humanity)

Cost one "Food" one "Energy"

Zombie Names:

_____
_____
_____
_____
_____
_____
_____
_____
_____
_____
_____

Reward Total:

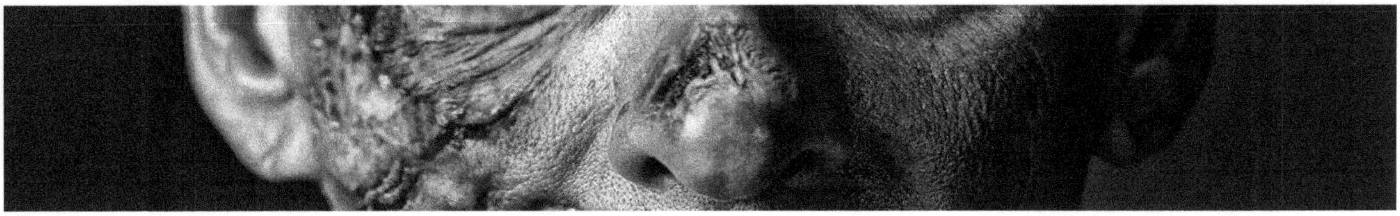

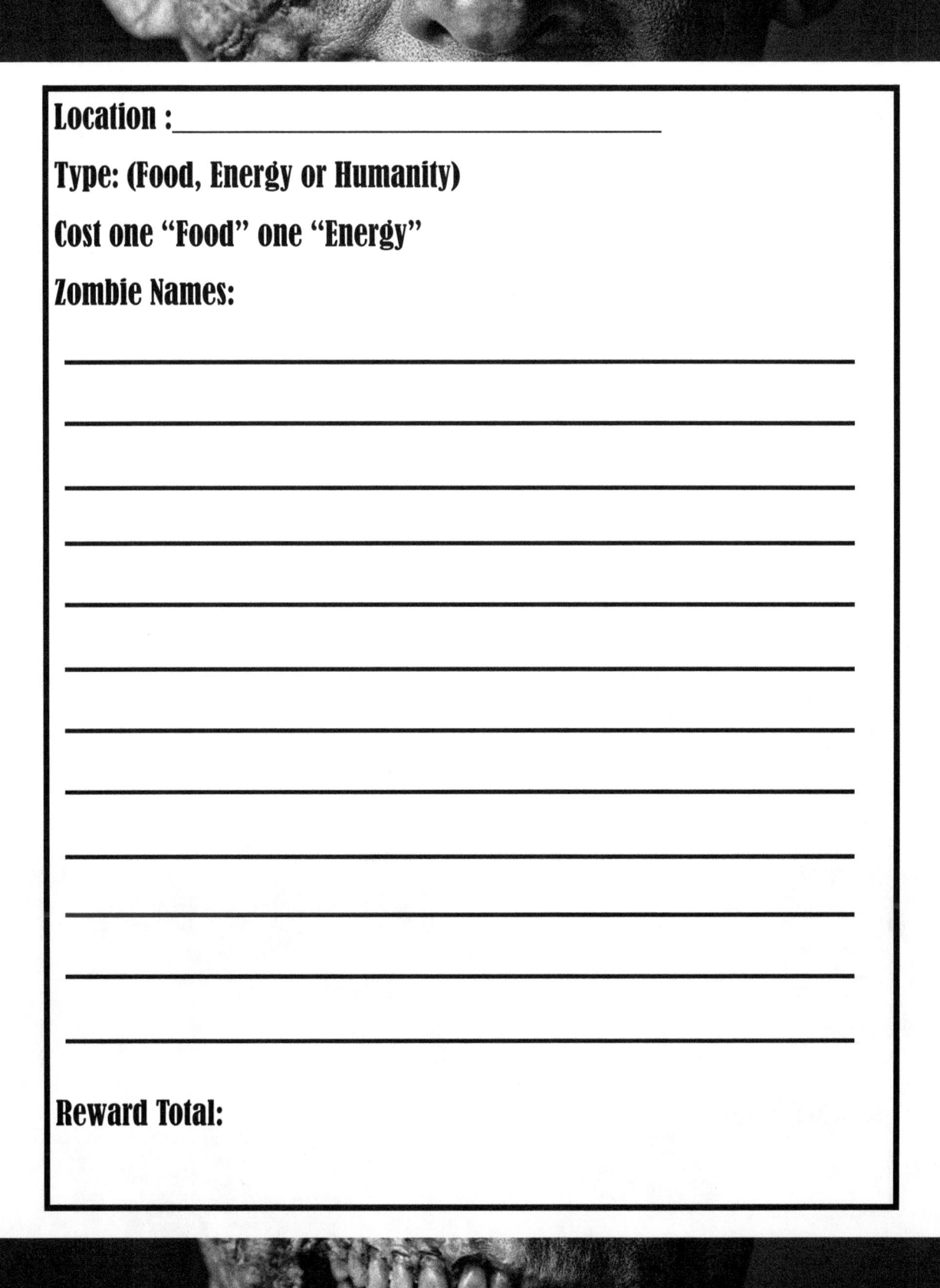

Location :_____

Type: (Food, Energy or Humanity)

Cost one "Food" one "Energy"

Zombie Names:

_____

_____

_____

_____

_____

_____

_____

_____

_____

_____

Reward Total:

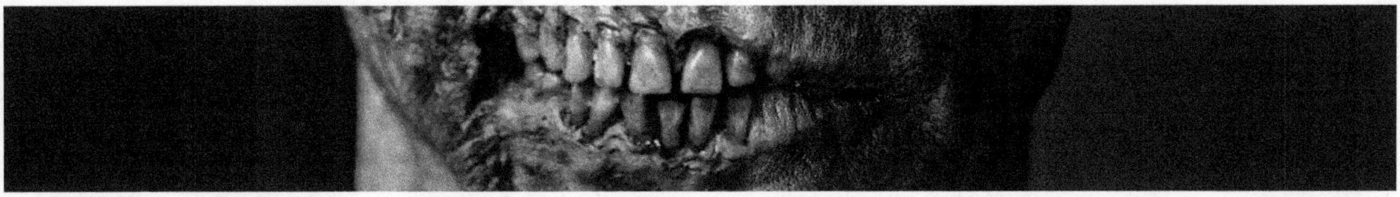

Location : _____

Type: (Food, Energy or Humanity)

Cost one "Food" one "Energy"

Zombie Names:

_____

_____

_____

_____

_____

_____

_____

_____

_____

_____

_____

Reward Total:

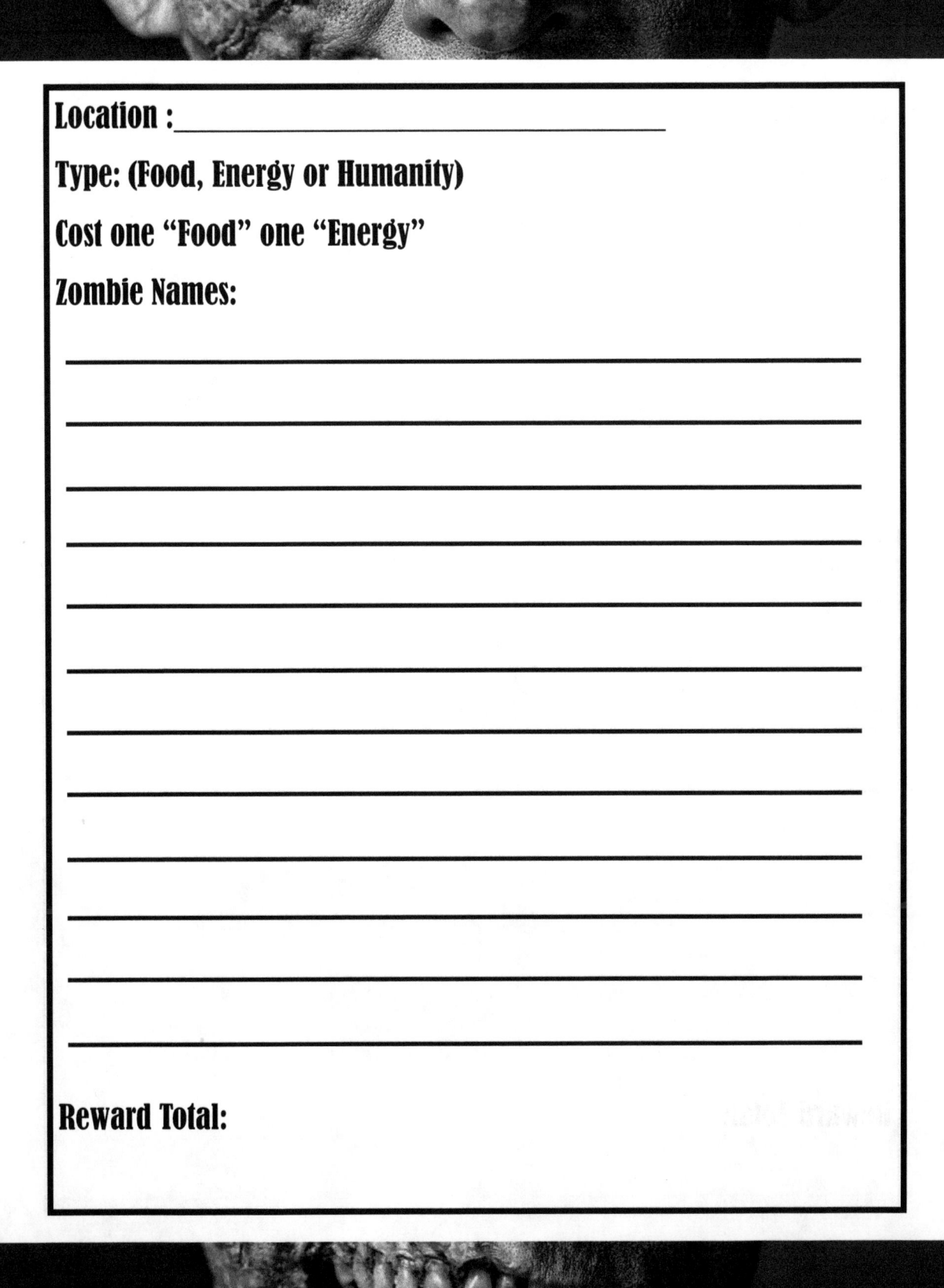

Location :_____

Type: (Food, Energy or Humanity)

Cost one "Food" one "Energy"

Zombie Names:

_____

_____

_____

_____

_____

_____

_____

_____

_____

_____

Reward Total:

Location : _____

Type: (Food, Energy or Humanity)

Cost one "Food" one "Energy"

Zombie Names:

_____

_____

_____

_____

_____

_____

_____

_____

_____

_____

_____

Reward Total:

Location :_____

Type: (Food, Energy or Humanity)

Cost one "Food" one "Energy"

Zombie Names:

_____
_____
_____
_____
_____
_____
_____
_____
_____
_____

Reward Total:

Location : _____

Type: (Food, Energy or Humanity)

Cost one "Food" one "Energy"

Zombie Names:

_____

_____

_____

_____

_____

_____

_____

_____

_____

_____

Reward Total:

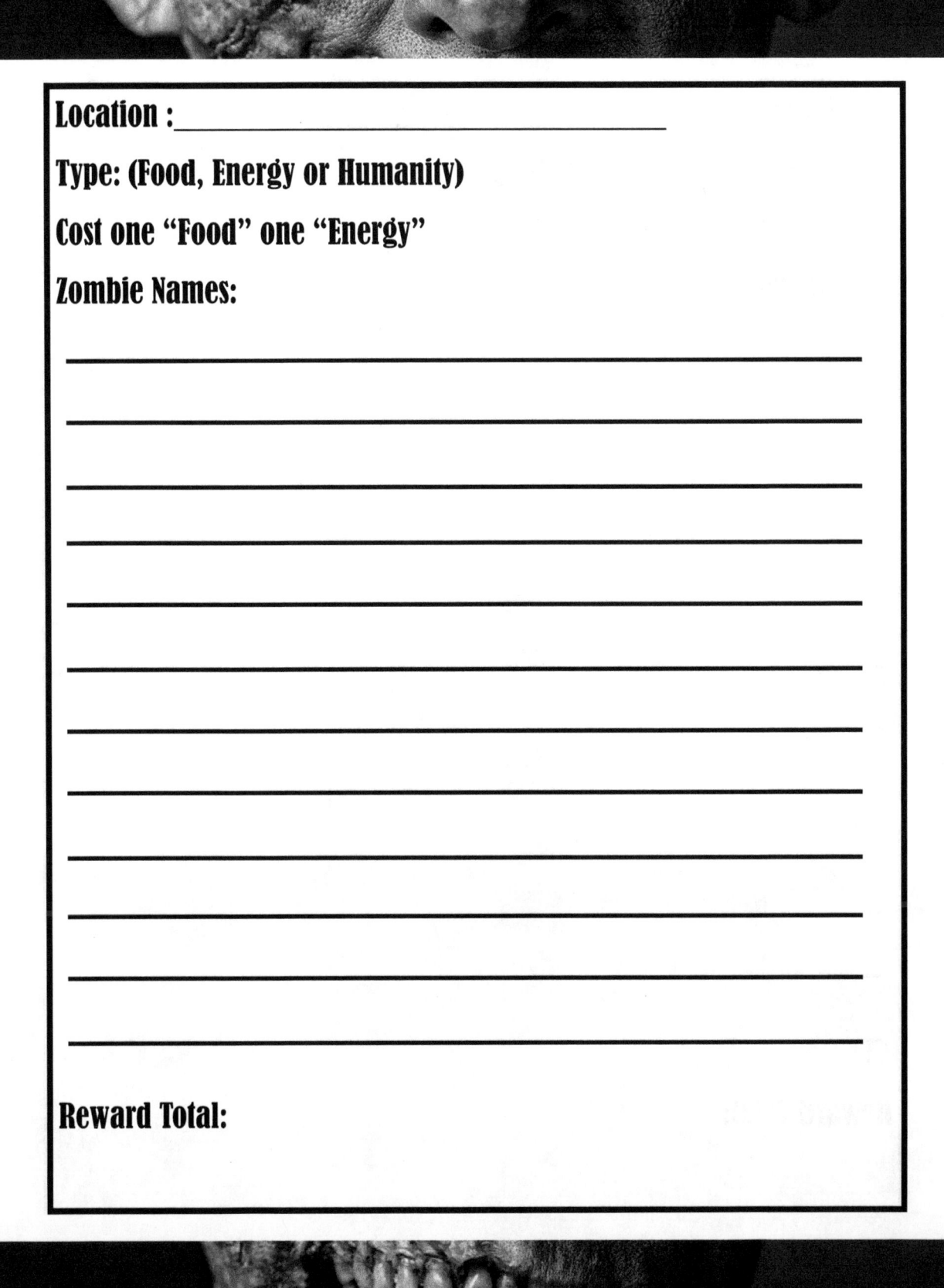

Location : _____

Type: (Food, Energy or Humanity)

Cost one "Food" one "Energy"

Zombie Names:

_____
_____
_____
_____
_____
_____
_____
_____
_____
_____
_____
_____

Reward Total:

Location :_____

Type: (Food, Energy or Humanity)

Cost one "Food" one "Energy"

Zombie Names:

_____
_____
_____
_____
_____
_____
_____
_____
_____
_____

Reward Total:

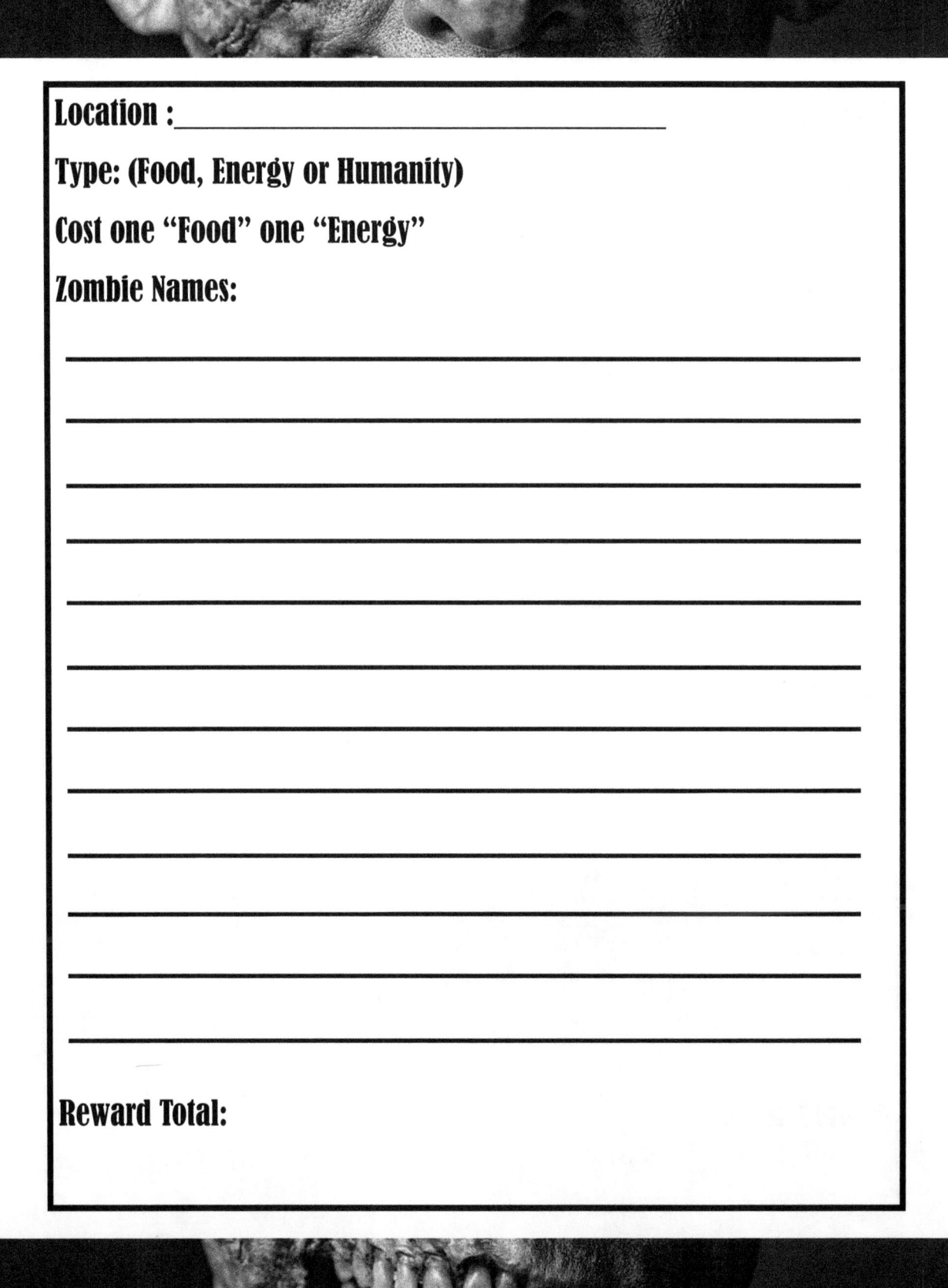

Location : _____

Type: (Food, Energy or Humanity)

Cost one "Food" one "Energy"

Zombie Names:

_____

_____

_____

_____

_____

_____

_____

_____

_____

_____

Reward Total:

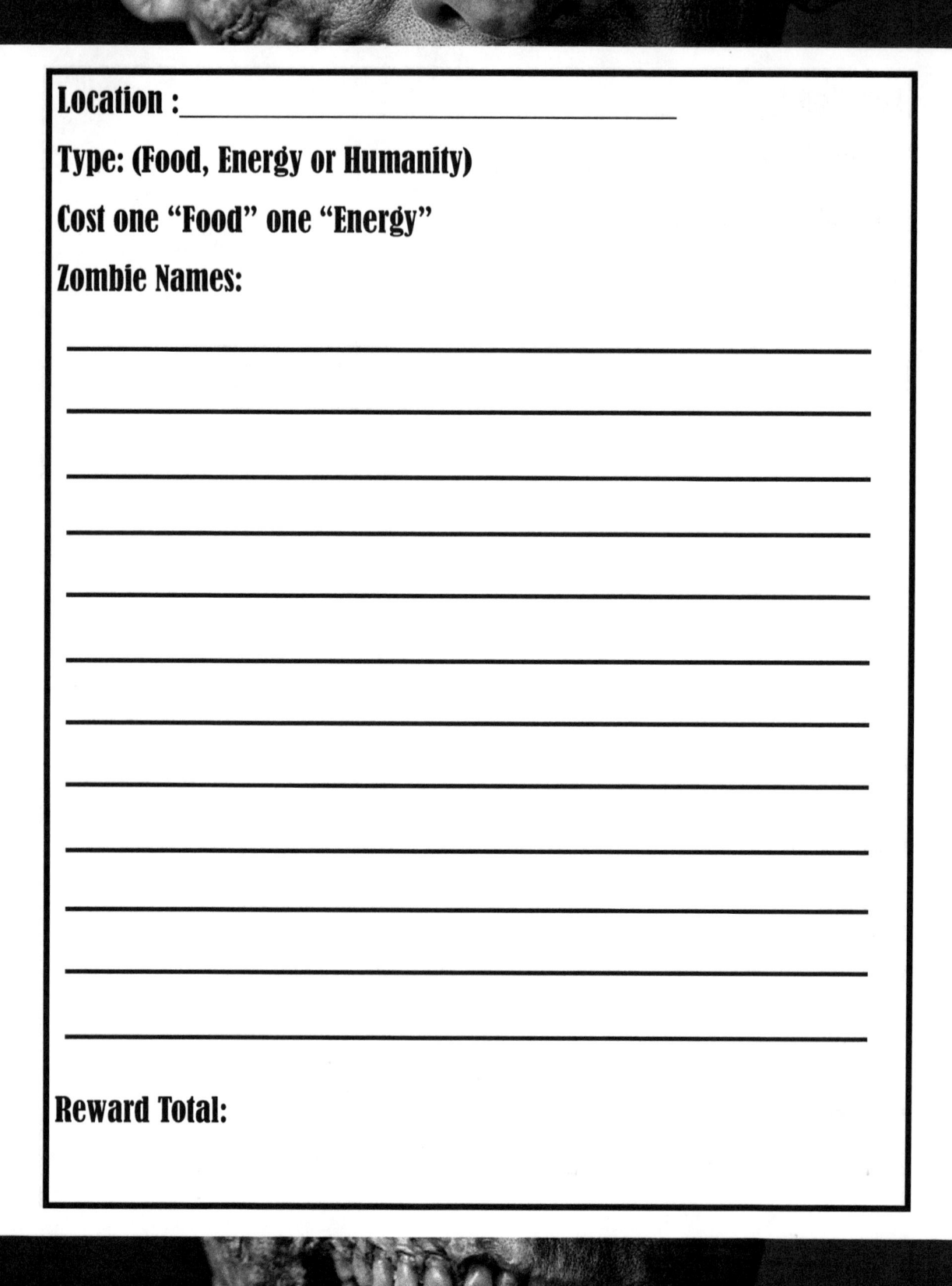

Location :_____

Type: (Food, Energy or Humanity)

Cost one "Food" one "Energy"

Zombie Names:

_____
_____
_____
_____
_____
_____
_____
_____
_____
_____
_____
_____

Reward Total:

Location :_____

Type: (Food, Energy or Humanity)

Cost one "Food" one "Energy"

Zombie Names:

_____
_____
_____
_____
_____
_____
_____
_____
_____
_____
_____

Reward Total:

Location : _____

Type: (Food, Energy or Humanity)

Cost one "Food" one "Energy"

Zombie Names:

_____

_____

_____

_____

_____

_____

_____

_____

_____

_____

Reward Total:

Location :_____

Type: (Food, Energy or Humanity)

Cost one "Food" one "Energy"

Zombie Names:

_____
_____
_____
_____
_____
_____
_____
_____
_____
_____

Reward Total:

Location : _____

Type: (Food, Energy or Humanity)

Cost one "Food" one "Energy"

Zombie Names:

_____
_____
_____
_____
_____
_____
_____
_____
_____
_____

Reward Total:

Location :_____

Type: (Food, Energy or Humanity)

Cost one "Food" one "Energy"

Zombie Names:

_____

_____

_____

_____

_____

_____

_____

_____

_____

_____

Reward Total:

Location : _____

Type: (Food, Energy or Humanity)

Cost one "Food" one "Energy"

Zombie Names:

_____

_____

_____

_____

_____

_____

_____

_____

_____

_____

Reward Total:

Location :_____

Type: (Food, Energy or Humanity)

Cost one "Food" one "Energy"

Zombie Names:

_____

_____

_____

_____

_____

_____

_____

_____

_____

_____

Reward Total:

Location : _____

Type: (Food, Energy or Humanity)

Cost one "Food" one "Energy"

Zombie Names:

_____

_____

_____

_____

_____

_____

_____

_____

_____

_____

_____

Reward Total:

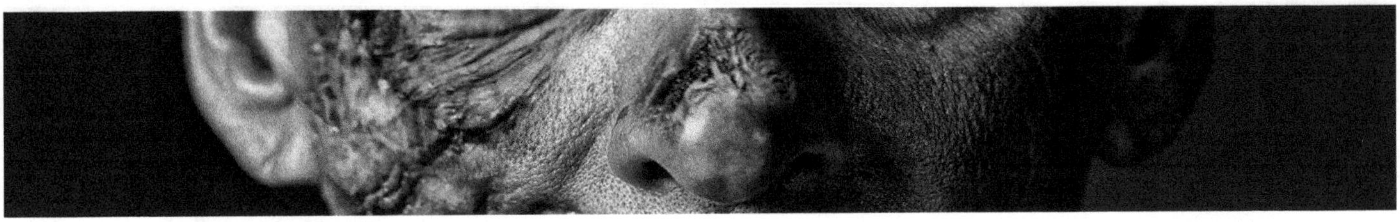

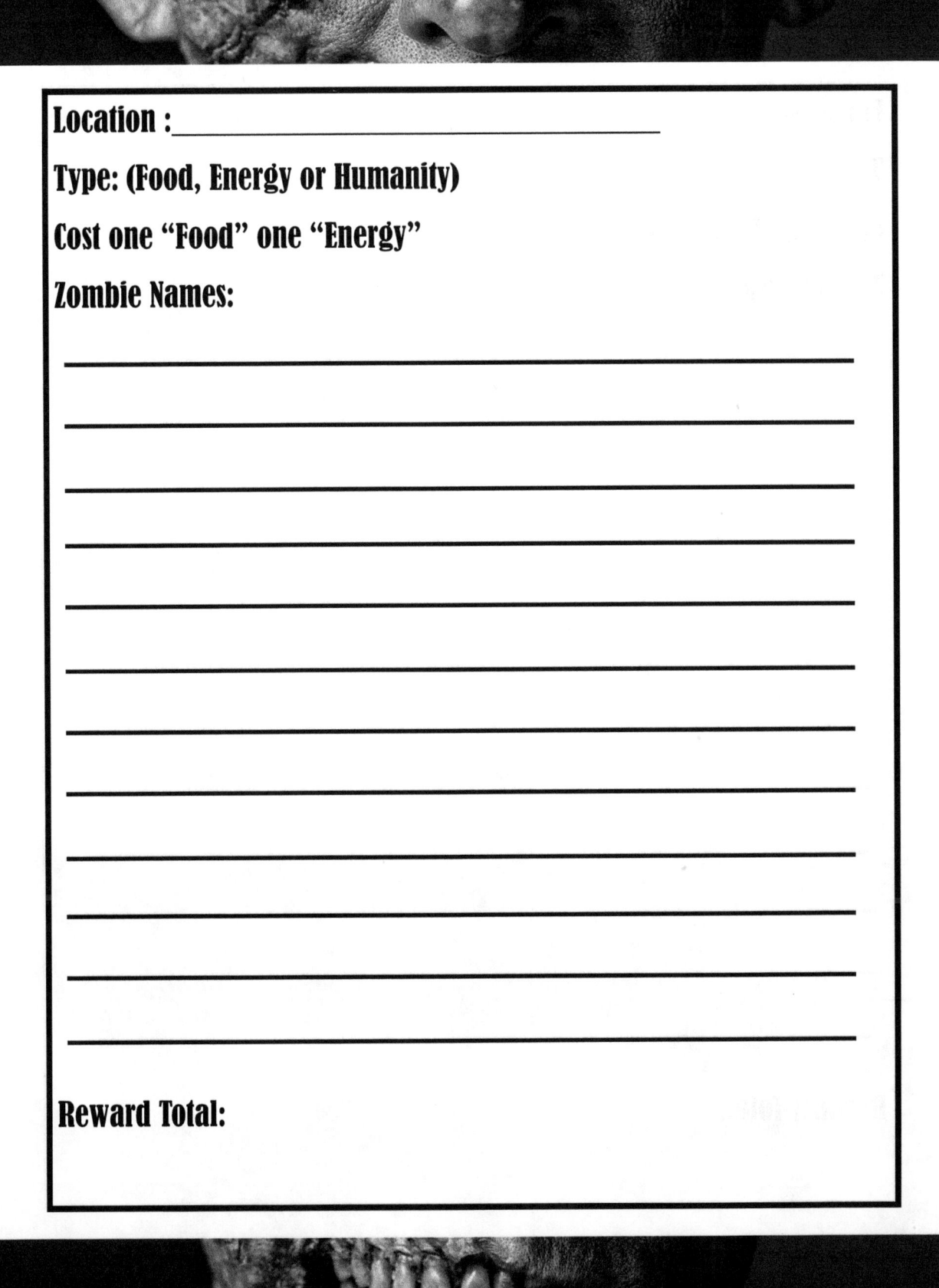

Location :_____

Type: (Food, Energy or Humanity)

Cost one "Food" one "Energy"

Zombie Names:

_____
_____
_____
_____
_____
_____
_____
_____
_____
_____
_____
_____

Reward Total:

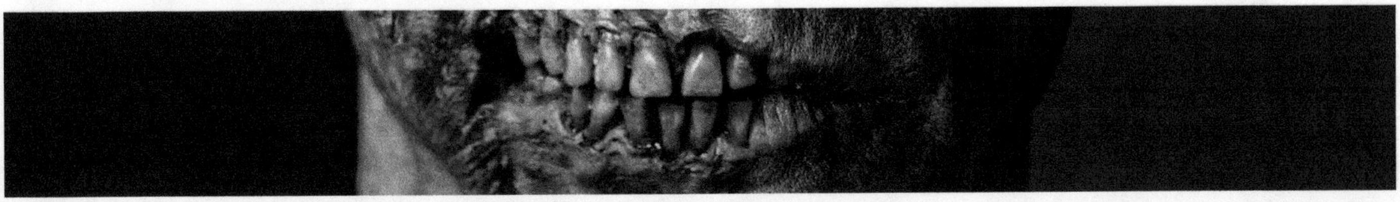

Location :_____

Type: (Food, Energy or Humanity)

Cost one "Food" one "Energy"

Zombie Names:

_____

_____

_____

_____

_____

_____

_____

_____

_____

_____

Reward Total:

Location :_____

Type: (Food, Energy or Humanity)

Cost one "Food" one "Energy"

Zombie Names:

_____

_____

_____

_____

_____

_____

_____

_____

_____

_____

Reward Total:

Location : _____

Type: (Food, Energy or Humanity)

Cost one "Food" one "Energy"

Zombie Names:

_____

_____

_____

_____

_____

_____

_____

_____

_____

_____

Reward Total:

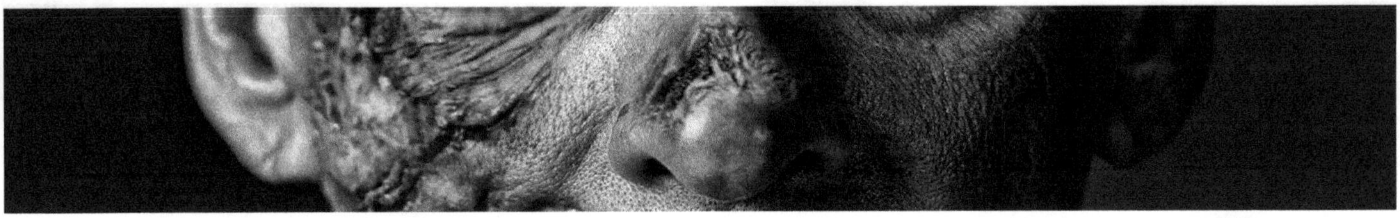

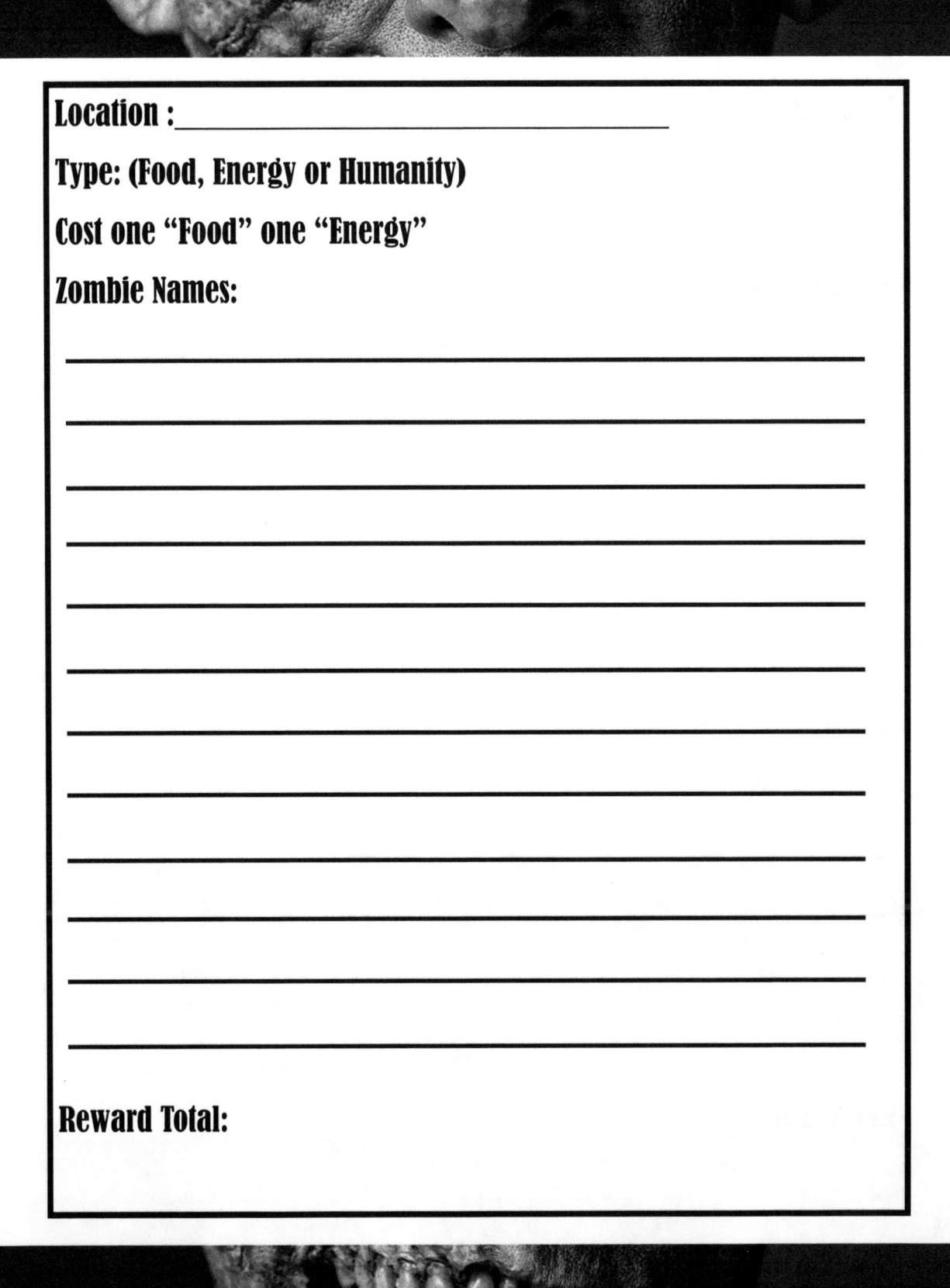

Location :_____

Type: (Food, Energy or Humanity)

Cost one "Food" one "Energy"

Zombie Names:

_____

_____

_____

_____

_____

_____

_____

_____

_____

_____

Reward Total:

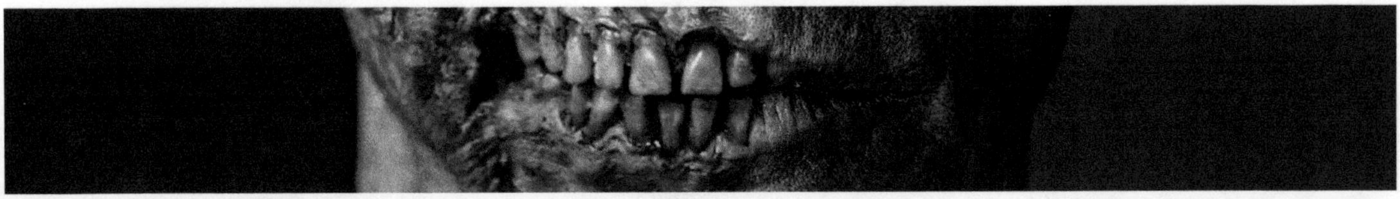

Location :_____

Type: (Food, Energy or Humanity)

Cost one "Food" one "Energy"

Zombie Names:

_____

_____

_____

_____

_____

_____

_____

_____

_____

_____

Reward Total:

Location : _____

Type: (Food, Energy or Humanity)

Cost one "Food" one "Energy"

Zombie Names:

_____

_____

_____

_____

_____

_____

_____

_____

_____

_____

Reward Total:

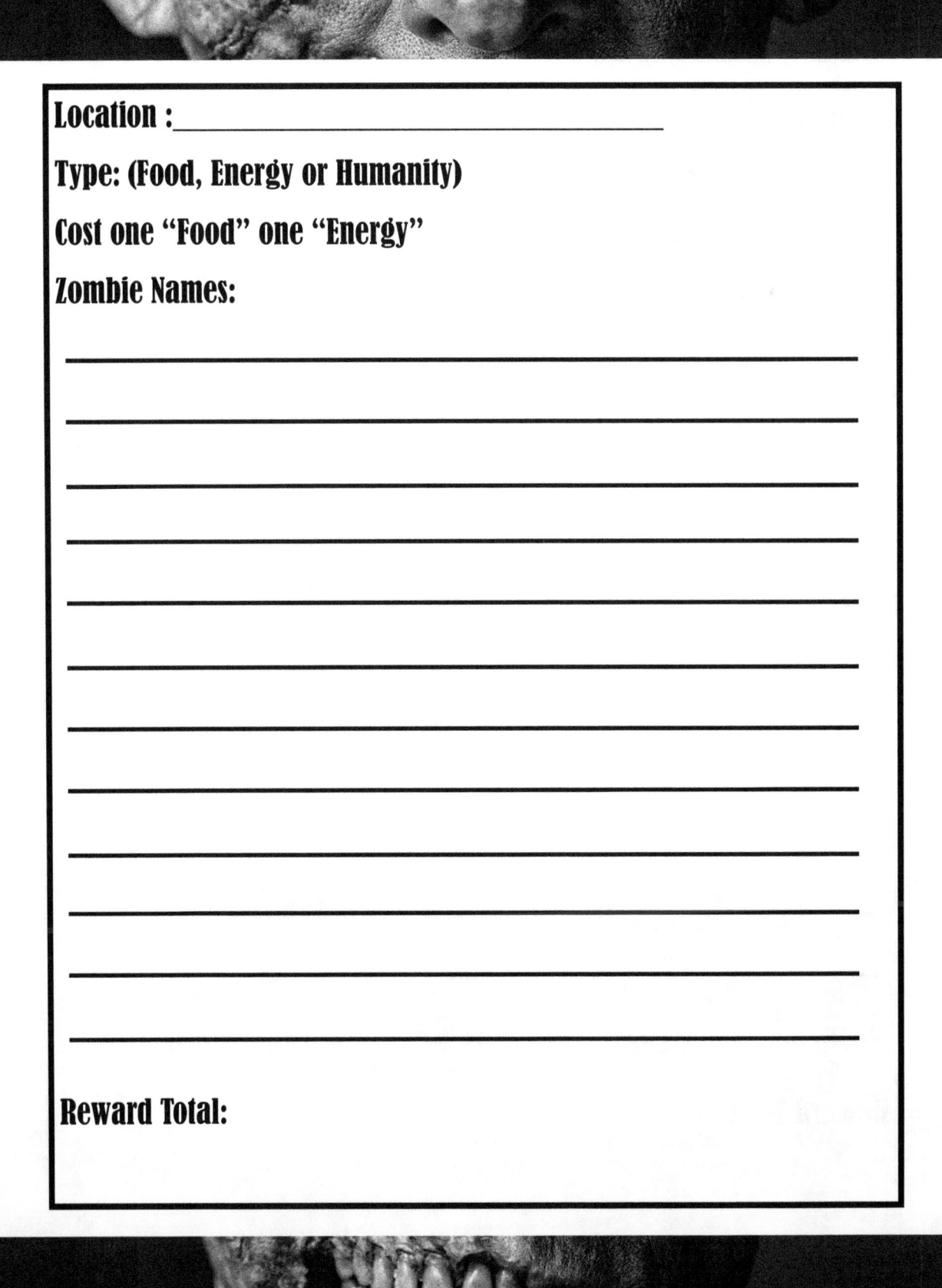

Location : _____

Type: (Food, Energy or Humanity)

Cost one "Food" one "Energy"

Zombie Names:

_____
_____
_____
_____
_____
_____
_____
_____
_____
_____

Reward Total:

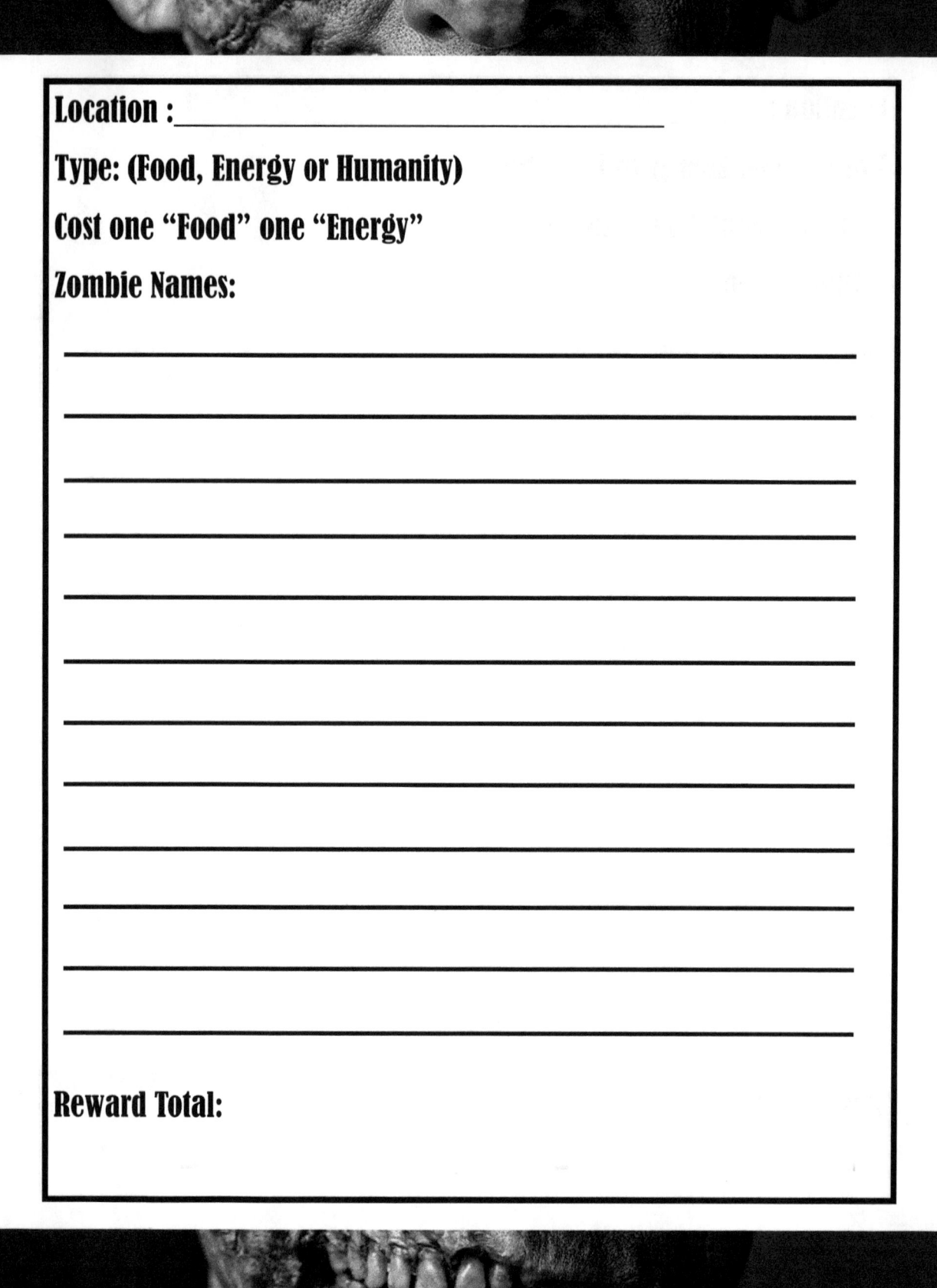

Location :_____

Type: (Food, Energy or Humanity)

Cost one "Food" one "Energy"

Zombie Names:

_____

_____

_____

_____

_____

_____

_____

_____

_____

_____

Reward Total:

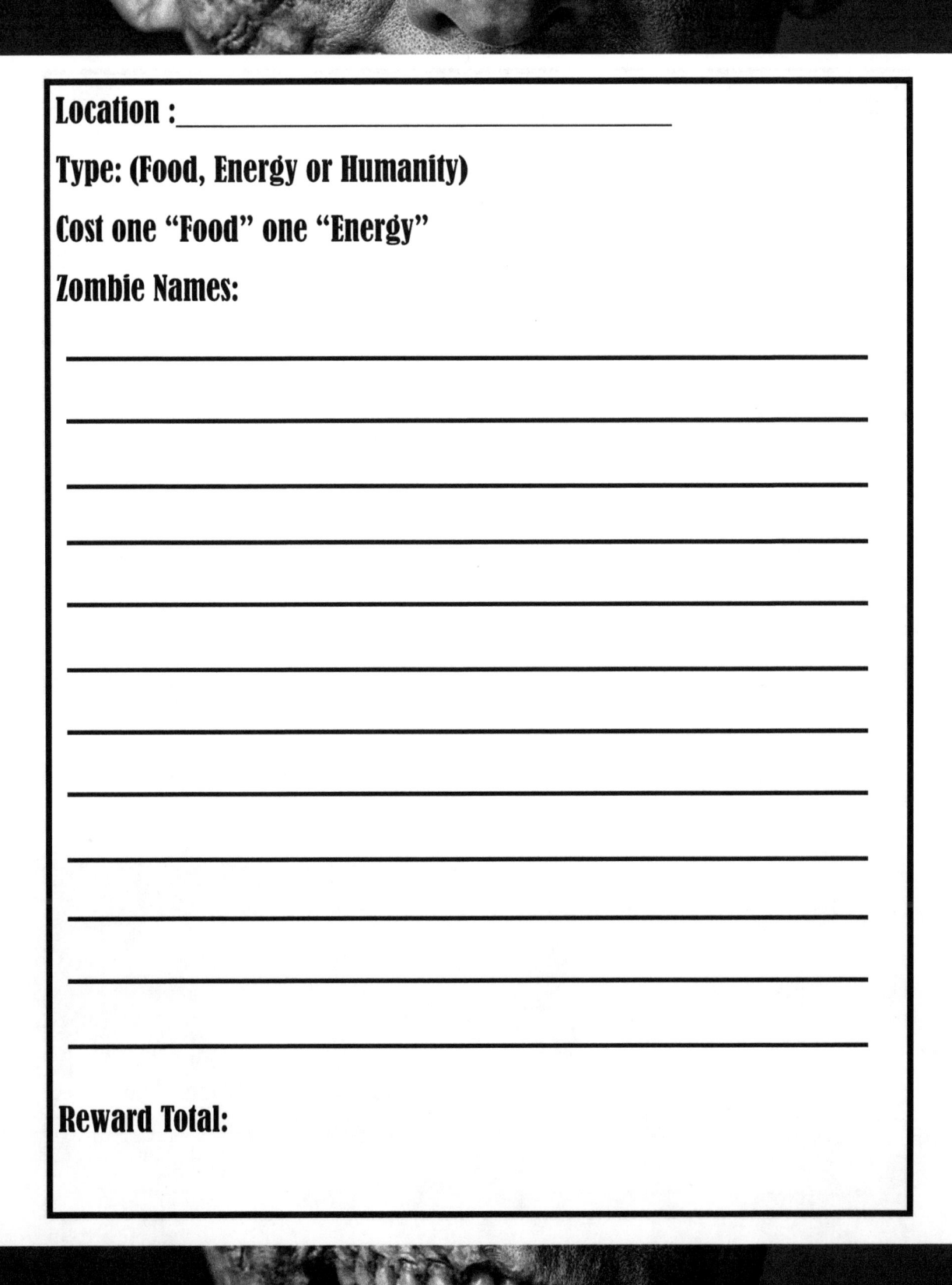

Notes:

Notes:

Notes:

Notes:

Notes:

Notes:

Looking for other travel guides?

Use the "interactive travel guide" search term on Amazon.com

Want to order 10 or more guides?

Have a business you would like to create a special page for?

Have a comment or city you would like to request?

Contact:

Johndavidpennington@yahoo.com

Interactive Travel Guide and Survival Games provide travel guides that specialize in giving you a fantasy frame for your vacation.

While we do suggest locations and activities that is only a small part of the guide. The majority of the guide gives you sheets to record your experience and play the game.

If you are looking for an informational travel guide this will only provide a small list of suggestions.

This game is designed for people looking for a new way to experience travel and make the most out of their experiences. This guide also gives you a reason to start up a conversation.

Enjoy!